Jerome Dean Davis

A Sketch of the Life of Rev. Joseph Hardy Neesima

Jerome Dean Davis

A Sketch of the Life of Rev. Joseph Hardy Neesima

ISBN/EAN: 9783337333904

Printed in Europe, USA, Canada, Australia, Japan

Cover: Foto ©Lupo / pixelio.de

More available books at **www.hansebooks.com**

A SKETCH OF THE LIFE

OF

REV. JOSEPH HARDY NEESIMA, L.L.D.,

PRESIDENT OF DOSHISHA, KYOTO,

PREPARED BY

REV. J. D. DAVIS, D. D.,

PROFESSOR OF THEOLOGY IN DOSHISHA.

"FOR ME TO LIVE IS CHRIST, TO DIE IS GAIN," PHIL. I. 21.
"FOR NONE OF US LIVETH TO HIMSELF, AND NONE DIETH TO HIMSELF." ROM. XIV. 7.

TOKYO:

FOR SALE BY

Z. P. MARUYA & Co., LIMITED;

YOKOHAMA, SHANGHAI, & SINGAPORE,

KELLY & WALSH, LIMITED.

Printed at the "Seishi-Bunsha."

1890.

PREFACE

The life, character and work of our brother who was so recently "called up higher," were remarkable and unique; much of his life was spent in our midst here in Kyoto. For over fourteen years, it was my privilege to be very intimately associated with him, and I have been asked to prepare a brief sketch of his life which may perhaps serve as an introduction to larger works which will doubtless be published later both in Japan and in the United States.

In preparing this sketch, I have consulted Dr. Neesima's diary, written before he left his home for Hakodate, while on the voyage thither, and in Hakodate, up to the day he sailed from that place on his great quest for truth, and also a copy of the brief sketch of his life, written by the late Miss Phebe Fuller McKeen, one of his sabbath school teachers; this sketch was written after Dr. Neesima had been in Phillips Academy, Andover, Mass., about a year. I have quoted freely from the latter in the first chapter and the beginning of the second, using Dr. Neesima's own words in broken English which he wrote out, or which his teacher above referred to, copied from his lips before he had had an opportunity to master the English language. I have also quoted from his journal written on his trip around the world in 1884, 5; I also quote freely from letters received from our brother during the last fifteen years, and I give in some detail the history of the founding of the Doshisha Schools, the great work of Dr. Neesima's life.

His presence with us has been a blessing, and his memory is a benediction to us all. My hope and prayer is that God may use this sketch for his own glory in the advancement of his Kingdom in Japan.

Doshisha, Kyoto, February, 1890.

J. D. Davis.

CONTENTS.

	PAGE.
Chapter First; Birth, Early Surroundings and Start from Japan...	1
Chapter Second; Trials and Preparation ...	17
Chapter Third; Laying Foundations ...	39
Chapter Fourth; Marriage, Trials, Work ...	55
Chapter Fifth; Broadening Plans; Tour Abroad ...	81
Chapter Sixth; Last Days of Work; Sickness, Death and Burial...	129
Chapter Seventh; Meditations, Character, Lessons...	143

I.
BIRTH, EARLY SURROUNDINGS AND START FROM JAPAN.

"*Now the Lord said unto Abram, Get thee out of thy country, and from thy kindred, and from thy father's house, unto the land that I will show thee.*"　　　　　Genesis, XII. 1.

"*God moves in a mysterious way.*
"*His wonders to perform.*"　　　Cowper.

"*Faith is nothing else but the soul's venture.*" W. Bridge.

　　　　　　　　　　　　　　Rashly,
"*And praised be rashness, for it,—let us know,*
"*Our indiscretion sometimes serves us well,*
"*When our deep plots do pall; and that should teach us,*
"*There's a divinity that shapes our ends,*
"*Rough hew them how we will.*"
　　　　　　　　Shakespeare.

Wife.   Wife's mother.   Father.   Mother.   Sister.

CHAPTER FIRST.

The ancestors of Mr. Neesima were of the samurai class, the retainers of a Daimio of Joshu, an interior province, with the Daimiate at Annaka about seventy five miles from Tokyo. His father, however, lived with his lord in Tokyo at the time of Mr. Neesima's birth and until after he went away to America. His father taught a school for the boys among the families of the retainers, and also assisted in keeping the accounts and in other writing in the office of the Daimio.

Mr. Neesima was born in Tokyo, January 14th, 1843. He was ten years old when Com. Perry first entered the bay of Yedo. He was early taught to read and write Chinese, and later, the sword exercise. He was also taught to worship the family gods which stood upon the shelf of a room in the house. From the time he was about fifteen years old, however, he refused to worship these idols. He could see for himself that they were only "whittled ones" and that they never touched the food and drink which he offered them. The family consisted, besides himself, of a younger brother who died while he was in America, and four sisters, only one of whom survives. Mr. Neesima's father died three years ago, and his mother still lives at the age of eighty-four.

The quotations below are from Mr. Neesima's imperfect English, as copied by Miss Mc Keen before he had been in America a year.

About the time he was sixteen years old, he was going into his study of the Chinese language with great enthusiasm when his prince, "picked up me to write his daily book, although it would not had been my desire, I was obliged to go up his office." A new light dawned upon him about this time. "A day my comrade sent me a Atlas of United States, which was written in Chinese letter by some American minister. I read it many times, and I was wondered so much as my brain would melted out of my head, because I liked it very much; picking one president, building free schools, poor-houses, house of correction and machine working, and so forth, and I thought that a government of every country must be as President of United States, and mourned myself that a governor of Japan, why you keep down us, as a dog, or a pig? We are people of Japan; if you govern us, you must love us as your children. From that time I wished to learn American knowledge, but, alas! I could not got any teacher to learn it. Although I would not like to learn Holland, I was obliged to learn it, because so many of my countrymen understood to read it."

But it was difficult for him to find time for the study of Dutch. "Once when his prince had, for the second time, caught him running away from the office, to go to his Dutch teacher, and had given him a flogging for it, he asked, ' Why you run out from here again'? When I answered him that 'I wish to learn foreign knowledge, because foreigners have got best knowledge, and I hope to understand very quickly; therefore, tho I know I must stay here and reverence your law, my soul went to my master's house to learn it, and my body was obliged to go thither too.' Then he said to me very kindly, 'You can write Japan very well, and you can learn yourself enough with it; if you don't run away from here any more, I will give you more wages. With what reason will you like foreign knowledge? Perhaps it will mistake yourself.' 'I said to him sooner, why will it mistake myself? I guess every one must take some knowledge. If a man has not any knowledge, I will worth him as a dog or a pig.' Then he laughed and said me 'You are a stable boy.'"

"This was not the only time that thirst for knowledge brought him both ridicule and blows. His family and acquaintances thought him very foolish to be craving needless knowledge, still he , never took care to them,' and; 'held his stableness very fast.' His work increased, however; so that he had no time for study and this cost him 'many musings in my head'; and at last he became fairly sick with thwarted purposes and unsatisfied longings. After various efforts to cure him, his physician told him, 'Your sickness comes from your mind; you must try to destroy your warm mind, and must take walk for the healthfulness of your body, and it would be more better than many medicine.' 'My prince gave me plenty times to feed my weakness, and my father gave me some money to play myself'; all of which he devoted to the study of Dutch, and 'a small Book of Nature' which fell into his hands, delighted him so much that it proved, 'more better to my sickness than doctor's medicines.'"

So health came back, and with it came the busy days and studious nights. In his Book of Nature he met with some things he was unable to understand, because he had never studied Arithmetic, so he went to an Arithmetic school until he had mastered enough to go through his Book of Nature intelligently. "Here are some reflections of this young seeker after knowledge in his own words. 'Some day I went to the seaside of Yedo, hoping to see the view of the sea. I saw largest man of war of Dutch lying there, and she seemed to me as a castle, or as a battery, and I thought, too, that she would be strong enough to fight with enemy. While I look upon her, one reflection came upon my head, that we must open navy, because my country is surrounded by water, and if foreigners fight to my country, we must fight with them at sea, but I made other reflection, too; that, since foreigners trade, price of everything get high, the country get poor; therefore, because the countrymen don't understand to do trade with foreigners, therefore we must know to do trade, and we must learn foreign knowledge. But the government's law neglected all my thoughts and I cried out myself, 'Why government? why not let us be free? why let us be as a bird in a cage, or as a rat in a bag?'"

"So he set to work in a government marine

school, whenever he could get away from his work, seeking information which he might turn to account for his country in the future. He had just made a good beginning in navigation when night study injured his eyes so that he was obliged to leave books entirely for a year and a half, ' Which would not come again in my life.' He had hardly recovered from this trouble so as to resume his place in his prince's office, when he was beset with measles, and his eyes, in consequence, ' began to spoil again,' so that he was obliged to spend many times very vainly." " When he did begin to use his eyes again, however, it was to some purpose. ' A day I visited my friend, and I found out small Holy Bible in his library, that was written by some American minister in China language and had shown only the most remarkable events of it. I lend it from him and read it at night. I was afraid the savage country's law, which if I read the Bible, will cross ' i. e. crucify, ' my whole family.' "

" This abridgement of the Bible contained little but the grand facts of creation and redemption, and these were entirely new to this earnest young soul who pored over its pages." The opening sentence of this book was, " In the beginning

God created the heavens and the earth." "He says, 'I put down the book and look around me, saying. I Who made me, my parents? No, my God. God made my parents and let them make me. Who made my table? A carpenter? No, my God. God let trees grow upon the earth; although a capenter made up this table, it indeed came from trees; then I must be thankful to God, I must believe him, and I must be upright against him.'" He at once recognised his Maker's claim to love and obedience and began to yield them; he prayed, "Oh! if you have eyes look upon me; if you have ears listen for me." It was a long time after this, however, that he first learned to pray as a man talketh with his friend.

"From this time his mind was fulfilled to read English Bible, and he 'burned to find some teacher, or missionary,' who could teach him."

"His father was disturbed by his boy's new notions and certain that he would get the whole family into trouble, and on asking permission of his prince and his parents to go to Hakodate, where he hoped to meet some Englishman or American, he got not only a refusal, but a flogging. Still, 'my stableness did not destroy by their expostulations.' He next applied to a relative of his prince, a noble, higher in authority and rank than he, and got leave from him to go in one of his prince's vessels to Hakodate." Now he had gained his point, neither his father nor his prince could prevent him.

This was in March 1864, and when he heard this news, he exclaimed, "Oh heaven does not cast me off, the great point of my business is in this one thing," and he jumped for joy. He went to his room, divided up his things and packed up a bundle of those he wanted to take with him, but he could not sleep at all till morning, and on March 11th, old style, "with great pain but with a resolute heart, he left his family in tears and started on his search for truth, 'not thinking, that when money was gone, how would I eat and dress myself, but only casting myself on the providence of God.'"

On the 13th, the ship sailed away from the harbor and he was on the great ocean. He had told his mother, that he would be gone a year, he thought, but he little suspected then, that it would be more than ten years before he would again see his native city, and look into the faces of those he loved. His diary for the next seven weeks is intensely interesting. The sailing junk in which he went, stopped at many of the principal towns, along the coast, as Uraga, Sendai, Kumagasaki, etc., to survey the harbors, or to escape storms. Our young voyager was now twenty-one years old, and he made good use of his time in seeking for all the information possible about each of these places. His diary contains a minute description of each one of them, a map of the harbor, the governor's name, the number of counties into which the province is divided, if a castle town, the condition of the castle, and the history of the province; the size of the town, its taxes, whether light or heavy, the productions of the place, what kinds of woods are produced, what kinds of fish are exported, etc., etc.

He is surprised at the great abundance of the rice-whisky, or sake, which was retailed at three cents a quart. There was one other item which he recorded in this diary concerning these places, which I wish those foreigners, who, after a brief residence in Japan, go home and report that its morality is superior to that of Christian lands, could read or see for themselves. His picture of the number of prostitutes in these trading towns is a fearful one, too fearful, some of it, to reproduce here. In one of these towns, he says there were from two to four of these women in each house in the town; he was greatly astonished and shocked at it himself, although he freely indulged in sake drinking with his comrades while in these harbors.

April 21st, old style, he reached Hakodate, then an open port, with English, American and Russian consulates in it. Young Neesima was, however, doomed to disappointment at first, as he sought in vain for any teacher of English, and his small funds melted away very fast and he was obliged to look about him for means to feed the outer man, as well as the inner. In this he was successful, as he fell in with Père Nikolai, the Russian priest who has since so successfully taught the religion of the Greek Church, in Japan. Nikolai was glad to secure his services as a teacher of Japanese, so he removed to Nikolai's house, and began his work.

He found a few wide awake young Japanese among the acquaintances he made, and among them a clerk in an English store who could speak English tolerably well, and who played a most important part in the next great act in the drama of Neesima's life. As he met with these young friends from time to time, and told them of his intense desire to learn foreign

In Hakodate, 1864.

knowledge, they encouraged him, and on account of the great difficulties connected with learning it in Japan, the idea came to young Neesima's mind of leaving the country altogether. The more he saw of his native land, the more he longed to be able to "'bring a light into the darkness'; but it was a very serious question; if he left the country, death would be his only welcome back. To go was to adventure himself, a penniless wanderer with an unknown tongue, into a vast mysterious world of which he only knew that truth was there. Worst of all, it would bring grief and fear, possibly danger and death, into the home he loved." He spent much time in thinking over this momentous question; he discharged his duty as a teacher to Pere Nikolai faithfully, and as his employer went every day to the Russian hospital to have his eyes treated, young Neesima went with him, and in his diary, he describes in minute detail, all the appointments of this hospital, its buildings, its beds, its diet, its medicines, and most of all, the fact that the poor were treated without money and without price, made a deep impression upon his mind. The more he studied over the great question, the more he felt impelled to leave his country; he even gradually found reasons to justify him in going, notwithstanding the strong filial ties which bound him to his parents and friends. "He says, 'One reflection came upon my head, that, although my parents made and fed me, I belong indeed to heavenly Father; therefore I must believe him and I must run in his way: then I began to search some vessel to get out from the country.'"

If every soul was as loyal to truth as was this one, as earnestly seeking it, as loyally obeying and following it, this world would soon become the very gate of heaven indeed. The young friend in the foreign store who could speak English finally secured for Neesima a passage in an American schooner bound for Shanghai. It was necessary to get away with the utmost secrecy. He made all his arrangements, picked out a small bundle of his clothes which he could carry on his back; he had a letter written, purporting to come from his brother in Tokyo, saying that his father was very sick, and that he must hurry home. Providentially, Pere Nikolai had gone away out of town, but he showed the letter to his servants and to some others and removed all his goods to a friend's house. Toward evening, he took his little bundle of clothes and met his three friends for the last

Dressed as a servant.

time that evening. They had a supper together, passed around the sake cup in token of friendship, Neesima wrote a short poem, all wished him well and wished they were going too, and bade him good bye. Thus the hours were spent until near midnight, when our young hero, dressed as a servant, with his bundle on his back, sallied out into the darkness, following one of his friends who was dressed as a samurai with his two swords in plain sight. They wended their way by back streets down to the water's edge in a lonely spot, where his friends had a small boat waiting for him; he was placed in the bottom of the boat and covered up, with orders to appear as a woman who was being taken out to the ship, if they were hailed. It was now midnight, "a whispered word of parting, hushed footsteps, the muffled dip of an oar, and the true hearted young patriot who went to seek light and blessing for his country, had stolen away from her shores like a culprit," and was on an American schooner. This was June 14th, 1864, old style, but July 18th, new style.

II.
TRIALS AND PREPARATION.

"Wherein ye greatly rejoice, tho now for a little while, if need be, ye have been put to grief in manifold temptations, that the proof of your faith, being more precious than gold that perisheth tho it is proved by fire, might be found unto praise and glory and honor at the revelation of Jesus Christ." I-Pet. I. 6, 7.

"A raveled rainbow overhead,
"Lets down to life its varying thread,
"Love's blue, joy's gold, and fair between,
"Hope's shifting light of emerald green:
"While either side, in deep relief,
"A crimson pain, a violet grief!
"Wouldst thou amid their gleaming hues
"Clutch after those and these refuse?
"Believe! as thy beseeching eyes
"Follow their lines and sound the skies,
"There, where the fadeless glories shine,
"An unseen angel, twists the twine,
"And be thou sure, what tint soe'er
"The sunbeams' broken rays may wear,
"It needs them all, that broad and white,
"God's love may weave the perfect light." Mrs. A. D. T. Whitney.

"Through black waves and stormy blast,
"And out of the fog-wreath dense and dun,
"Guided and held shall the vessel run,
"Gain the fair haven, night being past,
"And anchor in the sun." Susan Coolidge.

CHAPTER SECOND.

Our young friend was cordially received on board the schooner by the kind hearted Captain, but he could not sleep any that night, and in the early morning Japanese officials were seen coming to search the ship, to make sure that no Japanese was secreted on board. The Captain hid Mr. Neesima in his own private room, under a pile of clothes. The officers came, and searched the ship, even coming to the Captain's room, but our hero was not discovered, and the ship weighed anchor, spread her sails and moved out to sea.

And now our young exile began to think what he had done. He had written a long letter to his prince telling him of his decision, he had written another to his home friends, urging them not to mourn, that all would come out right; but as he passed out to sea, and saw the mountains of his loved land fade from his vision and disappear, very sad thoughts filled a very heavy heart. To add to his anguish, he was expected to do servile work on the ship, and as he had never done any such work, but had always had servants to wait on him, his samurai blood rebelled. Once or twice when he was rudely ordered by the sailors to do some menial work, he thought of seizing his sword and cutting down the men who seemed to be insulting him, but as he reflected that he could not thus realise his great purpose, he calmed his passions and meekly submitted to the indignity. Again, he had less than four dollars in money when he came on board, and this ship would only go as far as Shanghai. What should he do then?

"He had a very disagreeable passage to Shanghai, and he was there for ten days in great doubt and fear lest he should be betrayed and taken back to Japan; but finally, he had the joy of finding an American vessel bound for Boston. By much effort, he succeeded in making the Captain understand that he would be glad to do anything, and ask no other pay than to be taken to America, and, 'I begged him if I get to America, please let me go to a school, and take good education.' So the Captain took him as his own servant, dressed him in foreign costume," gave him the name, Jo, "and on the voyage taught him navigation and English."

"The voyage was a long and roundabout one, however, to the goal of his wishes. The Wild Rover sailed along the coast of China to Manila and Saigon, trading here and there for eight months, before turning towards home. While they lay in the harbor of Hongkong, Mr. Neesima found the New Testament in Chinese; he felt that he must have it, but how should he get it, since he had promised to ask the Captain for no money? He thought of his two swords, and he finally exchanged his short sword for the New Testament.

At last, sails were set for the West, and in four months from that time, the land of promise dawned upon our wanderer."

During his life of a year, on the Wild Rover, as Mr. Neesima told the writer, he began to read his New Testament in the Chinese language; it is hard work for an educated Japanese to read the Chinese books unless they have been pointed for Japanese eyes, as the arrangement of words in a sentence is very different in the two languages. He could only spell out the meaning, but he began at Matthew and read on in course through Matthew, Mark and Luke, and in the midst of the voyage he came to the sixteenth verse of the third chapter of John, "God so loved the world that he gave his only begotten Son, that whosoever believeth on him shall not perish but have eternal life," and this made a very deep impression upon him, and he felt that this was just such a Savior as he needed.

His faith and patience were sorely tried on the long voyage, and when he reached the harbor of Boston, it seemed to him as if he was to be baffled. "Directly after coming into port at Boston, the Captain hurried down to Cape Cod to see his friends, and for ten weeks, young Neesima was left, 'with rough and godless men who kept the ship,' doing hard, heavy work, such as he had never been accustomed to do. Besides this, everybody he met on the wharf frightened him; they told him, 'Nobody on shore will relieve you, because since the war, the price of everything got high; ah! you must go to sea again.' 'I thought too,' he says, 'that I must work pretty well for my eating and dressing, and I could not get in any schools before I could earn money to pay to a school. When such thoughts pressed my brain, I could not work very well; I could not read book very cheerfully, and I only looked around myself a long time as a lunatic.'

He made one great discovery, however, during this tedious waiting time, the Captain had given him a little money to amuse himself with on shore, and he had bought a Robinson Crusoe, which he found in a second-hand bookstore on Washington Street, and Robinson Crusoe first taught him that he might pray to his heavenly Father as to a present, personal friend. He had not yet fully mastered his New Testament in a foreign language. This shipwrecked Robinson Crusoe prayed in his distress, why might not he? So every night, after he went to bed, he 'prayed to the God, Please don't cast me away into miserable condition. Please let me reach my great aim.'

"How little we know when we pray how long our heavenly Father has been preparing to answer our prayers!" What comfort there is in the thought that both we, and our prayers, our needs, and their answers, were all present with God when he made his plan, and that he has been preparing from all eternity to answer our prayers in the best way!

"That God who had turned this boy's heart away from idols, who had inspired him to feel after him, if haply he might find him, who had said to him, 'Get thee out of thy country, and from thy kindred and from thy father's house, unto the land that I will show thee;' this same God had not neglected to prepare a place for him in the land of promise to which he had led him. He had brought the young wanderer across the seas in a ship belonging to one of his own children, straight to the hands of one whose joy it was to spend his strength and his wealth in the service of his Master."

When the owner of the ship, the Hon. Alpheus Hardy, was finally told by the Captain, of this bright young Japanese who had thus come in search of truth, he said to the Captain that he would provide some way for his support. "When I first heard these things from my Captain," said Mr. Neesima, "I jumped for joy, my eyes was fulfilled with many tears, because I was very thankful to him, and thought, 'God will not forsake me.'" Mr. Hardy met the young Japanese, later, and asked him what his name was. "The sailors called me Jo," was the reply. "You are well named," said Mr. H., "God has sent you to be a savior to your people." His benefactor little knew, when he spoke those words, how much of truth there was in them.

Mr. Hardy's first thought was to make of him a

Hon. Alpheus Hardy.

house servant and table boy, but he soon found that he was not fitted for this, and in the mean time Mrs. Hardy had asked him to write out the reasons why he had left his native land and come to America. He did so in his broken English, and when Mr. and Mrs. Hardy read those words, they felt that God had sent him, and they accepted the sacred trust, and decided to give him a thorough education.

He was placed in Phillips Academy at Andover, where he made the best use of his opportunities, and where for the first time he fully realised his sins and publicly accepted Christ as his Savior, uniting with the church of Christ. Who can doubt, however, that he was accepted of God before this, and that he would have been all ready to gladly bow before his Savior and worship him, if he had died in the midst of his long voyage in search of truth?

COPY OF A LETTER WRITTEN BY MR. NEESIMA WHEN HE HAD BEEN IN AMERICA LESS THAN A YEAR, TO THE JAPANESE FRIEND WHO HELPED HIM GET AWAY FROM HAKODATE.

Andover, Feb. 23, 1866.
Mr. Munokite; Dear sir;

I am very well through God's mercy. Since I commenced my hazardous adventure, I have spent many valuable days in hard work; oh! sometimes I had very miserable work; but this work I did not do for money but for true knowledge. When I called on him who made heaven and earth and sea and all that in them is, my sorrow turned into joy and my misery to success. Oh! I may surely say it is very wonderful and marvelous that such success has fallen on me. I passed through many thousand miles of water very safely without hurricane, tempest, or any trouble When I came to Boston the ship's owner, Mr. Alpheus Hardy, and the ship's Captain, Horace S. Taylor, relieved me from my miserable condition, and give me all things which I needed and sent me to the academy at Andover, Mass., to get an education, paying my board and all expenses.

I came to the house of Mr. Hidden,—he don't keep any boarder but me only,— and he and his sister care for me as much as for one of their own family, and I am very much enjoyed to stay here. Also I find a kind and religious man in Mr. Flint, a neighbor who was a teacher of some higher school for thirteen years. Every evening, he hears me recite in Arithmetic, that is named Eaton's Higher

School Arithmetic, and his wife explains to me the most holy and valuable book in the world, entitled the New Testament and tells about our Savior, Jesus Christ, who was sent down from his Father to enlighten the darkness and save sinners. In the academy I am studying Reading, Spelling, Grammar, and the same Arithmetic; also I have a Bible lesson every sabbath. All the teachers and scholars and many who know about me are interested in me and love me, and some give me things to please me. But these things they don't do for my sake, but for the Lord Jesus Christ.

O, dear friend, think you well who is Christ. The same is the Light which shines on the benighted and wicked world and guides us unto the way of salvation. The light of candle is blown away, but this is the true light of eternal life, and we can by no wise blow it out, and we may take this life through Jesus Christ. "For God so loved the world that he gave his only begotten Son, that whosoever believeth on him should not perish but have everlasting life. For God sent not his Son into the world to condemn the world, but that the world through him might believe." See John, third chapter, 16 and 17 verses, New Testament.

O, dear friend, I have nothing to repay your

kindness, but will send only, study the Bible, and my photograph. Please care for your health and study the book I have mentioned above. Oh, alas! it is not the country's law to study the Bible and worship our tender and merciful Father who made us, loved us and gave his only begotten Son, through whom we may be saved. But the law ought to be broken, because it is made by the devil, the king of the world. The world was not made by the devil, but by our true Father, who gave unto us his true law. Oh friend, whether then is right in the sight of God to hearken unto the devil more than unto God, please judge you.

If the fierce devil persecute you for righteousness' sake, don't trouble yourself, I am sure God will protect you from all evil, and though your body should be killed, your soul would be received unto him and you would dwell in the brightest place with eternal life. I would like, indeed, to go there with you.

Your Truly Friend,
Neesima Simata.

In due time he was ready for college and entered Amherst College, where he graduated in 1870. The statement of Pres. Seelye, when asked for testimonials for Mr. Neesima as he was about to return to Japan, will be a sufficient comment upon his faithfulness in college. Said the President, "YOU CANNOT GILD GOLD."

His faithfulness and thoroughness as a student, are shown by the fact that he had in his possession a pile of large books nearly two feet high, which are filled with lectures and notes which he copied or wrote out while he was in College and in the Theological Seminary.

He entered Andover Theological Seminary, and in the fall of 1871, when I was in attendance at the meeting of the American board at Salem, Mass., just before I sailed to Japan, Mr. Neesima elbowed his way through the great crowd and found me; and when I answered his eager question, that I was going to Japan, he seized my hand and with tears in his eyes, told me how glad he was to meet me, and he wished me a hearty godspeed, and said he hoped to go back too, before long.

In the winter of 1871-2, the second Japanese embassy, consisting of Messrs. Iwakura, Okubo, Kido, Ito and Tanaka, crossed the Pacific, and after being snowbound for a week at Salt Lake City, finally reached Washington. The embassy at once felt the need of some one to act as interpreter who could also help them in their search into the institutions of these foreign lands, especially education. Hearing of Mr. Neesima who had then been in America about seven years, they sent an imperial mandate to him to appear before them; he was greatly troubled at this message, but after much thought and prayer, he wrote back, that he was an outlaw, that death hung over his head for having left his native land, that he recognised no ruler but the King of heaven, but that if they would send him an invitation to come and meet them as a friend, he would come. They at once sent him such an invitation. Then the question of how to meet them arose in Mr. Neesima's mind. It had been the custom in Japan from time immemorial for a man to bow to the earth when meeting a superior and prostrate himself before him. Mr. Neesima finally decided to meet them in the American way and went on to Washington.

They received him kindly and told him what they desired of him. He told them that he could accept their offers and meet their desires only on condition that they make out and give him a formal pardon for having left his country, and also another paper giving him the privilege of teaching Christianity when he should return to his native land. They made out the two papers, sealed them with the imperial signet and gave them to him. This brought a new joy to Mr. Neesima's heart, he could now write to his loved ones at home; he could hear from them directly, and they could hear from him. He had not dared to write to them, or let them know of his welfare or whereabouts, lest they should be all put to death. The long silence and suspense were broken. The younger brother had been made the head of the house in place of the one who was not; this younger brother having no children had adopted a boy as his son, and later, the brother had died, so that this adopted son was the head of the house, and Mr. Neesima never regained his position again, but started a new house. Great was the joy of the whole family to hear that the long lost son was alive.

Mr. Neesima now spent a year with the Japanese embassy, visiting all the capitals of Europe with them, and devoting all his energies to help them gain the information they desired. His "stableness" and firm Christian principle shone out during this visit to Europe. In most European countries, the railroad trains run on the sabbath, the same as on any other day, and the embassy often travelled on that day; Mr. Neesima, however, never travelled with them on the sabbath. He told the writer that he always stopped off Saturday night, alone, and followed on after them on Monday. He spoke of one of these experiences, when he stopped off, in France, Saturday night among entire strangers, and not knowing French, he expected to have a lonely day, but he wandered about and succeeded in finding a place where a Christian service was being conducted, and entering, he found it was a communion service. He remained and partook of the communion with them, and although he could understand but very little he spoke of it as among the most blessed experiences of his life.

By his faithfulness and his conscientious adherence to principle, he gained the confidence of these men, a confidence which lasted till the day of his death; and when he came back to Japan and wished to start his school, these men were at the head of the government, and to his intimacy with them and their firm confidence in him, the Doshisha owes its existence.

Mr. Neesima's careful habit of looking into all the details of whatever came in his way to examine, and especially his great interest in education which had led him to make a careful examination of the common school system of the United States, had prepared him to be of invaluable service to the embassy and to his country. He examined the systems in several of the States, and wrote out a carefully prepared paper which was taken as the basis of the report which the embassy made on education, and which was afterwards modified and introduced into Japan, and is the foundation of the system of education in the empire to-day.

As the time drew near for the departure of the embassy from Europe, to return home by way of India, Mr. Neesima was pressed to accompany them to Japan and it seemed that it would be almost impossible for him to refuse to do so, but a severe illness coming on at this time, compelled him to remain behind, among strangers, until long after the Embassy had sailed for Japan, so that, on his recovery, he returned to his studies in Andover.

He was very retired and studious in his manner, although his intense thirst for knowledge would lead him to break over his reserve and seek information from his fellow students. He was greatly afflicted with rheumatism during his last year in the

Seminary, and he suffered from its effects at times during the rest of his life.

He graduated in the summer of 1874, and now the question of his return to Japan, what relation he should sustain to the American Board, his ordination, and his support, all came up for solution. It was finally decided that it was best that he should receive ordination, before leaving for Japan, and a Council of churches in the State where he had spent ten years, was called. He passed a very satisfactory examination and was ordained as an evangelist,— the first of his race to take upon himself this office. He was also appointed a corresponding member of the Japan Mission of the American Board. Mr. Hardy also arranged to have sent to Mr. Neesima each year what he needed for his support, so that he was placed above anxiety on that point.

He was now all ready to start back to his loved land and friends, but there was still one thing which weighed upon his heart; he had come to America and seen for himself the light of Christian civilisation; he had drunk deeply at the fountains of knowledge, and he felt an inexpressible longing to see such a fountain of true knowledge opened in his own land; he had not started on his world-wide quest for truth for himself; he came for the good of his people; should he go back with a full heart but with an empty hand? The same Hand which had so wonderfully led him to America and which had taken care of him there and given him such a preparation for his work, led him farther to make an appeal which other hearts were ready to second, and so begin an enterprise which should be indeed a blessing to his whole people.

I quote here from Mr. Neesima's own words, written in a letter, the last one in English, which his hand ever penned, written only a few days before his death. He says, "Fifteen years ago I had a day-dream to found a Christian college. I used to express my intense desire to found it, especially to raise up Christian workers, to Dr. Clark, secretary of the American Board, and also to some other friends, but none of them gave me any encouraging words. However, I was not discouraged at all. I kept it within myself and prayed over it.

In the fall of 1874, I was invited to attend the annual meeting of said Board which was held in Rutland, Vermont, to bid my last farewell to my friends. I was then ordered to appear on the platform on the very last day of the meeting. In the evening of the previous day, I called on Mr. and Mrs. Alpheus Hardy, my benefactors, and consulted with them about the advisability of my bringing out my long cherished scheme, that is, to found a Christian college in Japan, in my farewell speech. Mr. Hardy was rather doubtful about my attaining any success; however, I was rather insisting to do it, because it was my last chance to bring out such a subject to such a grand Christian audience. Then he spoke to me half smiling and in a most tender, fatherly manner, said, 'Joseph the matter looks rather dubious, but you might try it.' Receiving that consent, I went back to the place where I was entertained and tried to make a preparation for the speech. I found my heart throbbing and found myself utterly unable to make a careful preparation. I was then like that poor Jacob, wrestling with God in my prayers.

On the following day, when I appeared on the stage, I could hardly remember my prepared piece; a poor, untried speaker: but after a minute or two I recovered myself, and my trembling knees became firm and strong; a new thought flashed into my mind, and I spoke something quite different from my prepared speech. My whole speech must have lasted less than fifteen minutes;

Trials and Preparation. 37

while I was speaking I was moved with the most intense feeling over my fellow countrymen, and I shed much tears, instead of speaking in their behalf. But before I closed my poor speech, about five thousand dollars were subscribed on the spot to found a Christian college in Japan. That generous subscription of our American friends became the nucleus of the present Doshisha, which is now recognised as the best and largest Christian College in Japan".

It was entirely natural that the officers and friends of the Board should not have encouraged Mr. Neesima at this time to appeal for money to found a College in Japan; their work is an evangelistic work, and their efforts are constantly put forth to secure contributions enough for their regular work, and they must of necessity discourage special appeals. The hand of God, however, was evidently in the movement which led to the foundation of the school.

The writer has heard from many persons who were present at that meeting that it was a scene never to be forgotten; the intense earnestness of this young Japanese, as he spoke of the great blessings of a Christian education, which he had received, and pictured to them, with broken voice and overflowing eyes, the darkness and need of his own people; the evident nervousness of the Secretaries at the manly appeal which was made, for the speaker said, " I cannot go back to Japan without the money to found a Christian College, and I am going to stand here till I get it." Then Governor Page of Vermont arose and said, " Put me down for one thousand dollars." Dr. Parker of Washington followed with five hundred dollars. Mr. Hardy with five hundred, William E. Dodge with five hundred, and others with lesser sums, until nearly five thousand dollars were raised.

III.
LAYING FOUNDATIONS.

"Behold I lay in Sion for a Foundation, a Stone, a tried Stone, a precious corner Stone of sure Foundation: he that believeth shall not make haste." Is. XXVIII. 16.

"And not only so, but let us also rejoice in our tribulations: knowing that tribulation worketh patience; and patience, probation; and probation, hope: and hope putteth not to shame; because the love of God hath been shed abroad in our hearts through the Holy Ghost which was given unto us." Rom. V. 3-5.

"The good man does better than he knows."

"Fasten your soul so high that constantly,
"The smile of your heroic cheer may float,
"Above the floods of earthly agonies." E. B. Browning.

"God's glory is a wondrous thing,
"Most strange in all its ways,
"And of all things on earth, least like
"What men agree to praise.
"Oh, blest is he to whom is given
"The instinct that can tell
"That God is on the field, when he
"Is most invisible!
"And blest is he who can divine
"Where real right doth lie,
"And dares to take the side that seems
"Wrong to man's blindfold eye!
"Oh, learn to scorn the praise of men!
"Oh, learn to lose with God!
"For Jesus won the world through shame,
"And beckons thee his road.
"And right is right, since God is God;
"And right the day must win;
"To doubt would be disloyalty,
"To falter would be sin!"

Faber.

CHAPTER THIRD.

Mr. Neesima reached Japan on his return, in December, 1874. He found great changes had taken place during his ten years absence. The Mikado was reinstated, his capital was changed from Kyoto, where his ancestors had ruled for a thousand years, to Tokyo; the Daimios had relinquished their feudal rights, and the pensions of their retainers were capitalised; the Julian or Gregorian calendar had been adopted, and the sabbath was made a holiday; the Post Office with a Money Order system, a Savings Bank system and a Postal Delivery system were established; newspapers were being printed and circulated; an army and a navy on a foreign plan were formed; a mint was established; the coast was being surrounded with light houses; the first railroads were opened, and a network of telegraphs were unifying the old feudal kingdom. Most of these changes had taken place one or two years before Mr. Neesima returned. The great question of constitutional liberty was beginning to be agitated and the men whose confidence and love Mr. Neesima had gained in his intercourse with the embassy, three years before, were at the head of the Government. Their prejudices had been removed and their minds broadened by their intercourse with Western nations, and they were ready to encourage the adoption of Western civilization in their own empire.

Mr. Neesima was offered, again and again, places of high position under these men and urged to accept them, but he steadily declined them. He allowed nothing to turn him from the great purpose of his life to establish a Christian College in his native land.

Soon after landing in Yokohama, he visited his aged parents who had gone back to their native province and were living in Annaka. There were at this time small churches in Tokyo, Yokohama, Osaka and Kobe, but it was hardly safe to profess Christianity, even in the open ports. Away from the open ports there was very little, if any, effort on the part of any Japanese to teach the forbidden doctrines. But no sooner did Mr. Neesima reach Annaka, seventy-five miles from Tokyo, than the people began to beg him to tell all about foreign countries, and he took that opportunity to openly tell them about Christianity; he did this so boldly for several days that the Governor of that province became troubled. Mr. Neesima was plainly violating the old law, but yet he was no ordinary person; he had been attached to the Iwakura embassy and was already a widely known man. To arrest or even caution him might have some unknown results; so the Governor went hastily in person to Tokyo, and laid the matter before some of the men who were at the head of the government. They replied, "If it is Neesima, it is all right, let him alone," so the Governor returned satisfied, and the work was begun which resulted in the organisation of the Annaka church a few years later under the labors of Mr. Yebina, and the Annaka church, with the five other churches within a very few miles, which have sprung from it, make it probably the most thoroughly evangelised community in Japan. Several of the members of that provincial assembly and a majority of the standing committee are Christian men and two-thirds of the members of the Imperial Diet, elected from that province, are Christians. From the time of Mr. Neesima's visit to Annaka dates the entrance of Christianity into the heart of Japan, and that was the beginning of the fearless preaching of the gospel in the Interior. The same Count who gave to the Governor the reply mentioned above, himself told Mr. Neesima of this fact a short time afterwards.

After a few weeks spent with his friends in Annaka, preaching the Gospel, Mr. Neesima came on to Kobe and Osaka to confer in regard to the establishment of the Christian College.

A short time before Mr. Neesima's return, our Mission received a letter from Secretary Clark telling us that five thousand dollars were waiting to found a Collegiate and Theological training school to train Christian workers for Japan. We had not yet begun to think of such a school, or at least, we felt that it was far in the future; our first two churches had been organised that year, one in Kobe with eleven members, and one in Osaka with seven members; a few young men were found ready to listen to the truth, also, in Sanda, twenty miles from Kobe, but the villages about Kobe, and between Kobe and Osaka were so much opposed to Christianity that it was impossible to even teach a few men in a hotel, or tea house.

Mr. Neesima tried for several months to secure permission from the Governor of the Osaka-Fu to establish the College in that city; he saw the Governor many times and urged his plan; the Governor told him he would approve the establishment of the school there, but that no missionary should teach in it, so Mr. Neesima reluctantly gave up hope in Osaka, and then our thoughts were turned to Kyoto; but Kyoto was an interior city, where foreigners had never been allowed to reside; it had been the center of Buddhism and Shintoism in Japan for a thousand years, and, moreover, it was away from the centers of work which our Mission had opened.

The Mission, however, gave a reluctant consent to the location of the school in Kyoto, if permission could be secured, and in the summer of 1875, Mr. Neesima went to Kyoto, to see what could be done. The Lord had prepared the way before him; the city had been opened for one hundred days during the three previous years, while the exhibition was held there, and Rev. O. H. Gulick had spent three months in the city during the summer of 1872, and had made the acquaintance of Mr. Yamamoto Kakuma, a blind man who was then a private Counselor to the Kyoto Fu. Others of our Mission had met him during the next two summers and he had become greatly interested in

Christianity. When Mr. Neesima presented his plan for the establishment of a Christian College in Kyoto to Mr. Yamamoto, he was ready to give it his warm approval from the first, and he used his strong influence with the Governor of the Kyoto-Fu in the same direction, so that the Governor, also, gave his approval to the scheme.

The writer made a hasty visit to Kyoto in June of 1875 and, with Mr. Neesima, looked at a lot of land containing five and a half acres, 6500 tsubo, situated in the northern part of the city, just above the old palace grounds, and with a large temple grove of one hundred acres on the north side of it. This land was the former site of the palace of the Satsuma Daimio, the last resident being Shimadzu Saburo. It was now in the possession of the blind Yamamoto, and he gladly sold it to us for the school, for the sum of five hundred and fifty dollars.

Thus the site for the school was secured. What should be its name? Many names were thought of, but finally, the name, "Doshisha," was decided upon; this means one endeavor, or one purpose company. Mr. Neesima was in Kyoto all the summer of that year except during a hurried visit to Tokyo. Although the approval of the local

Laying Foundations.

government had been secured for the location of the school in Kyoto, the approval of the central government was necessary. A building must also be secured for the school and permission for a family to reside in Kyoto, and for a missionary to teach in the school. Mr. Neesima was busy with all these plans, and his heart was stirred also to find some way by which the Gospel could be freely taught in the school and in the city and all over the empire.

He writes, Aug. 2nd, "I had a most interesting interview with Mr. ———, a young man who is connected with the educational department at Tokyo. He told me that he will do his best to allow missionaries to be hired in our Kyoto school: but for teaching Christianity in it, he has no power to say much, because as Christian religion, it comes under Daikiyoin, or Department of Religion. I think it would not do for us to present this matter to Daikyoin, because they will never do us any favor. So I think a best way will be to try to get religious freedom in the empire. I will write to our influential men in the cabinet and induce them to work for it. Mr. ——— promised me to work for it privately among the radical statesmen. He rather asked me to come to Tokyo to see them myself.

In the first place I must get a letter from my native province which will assure the Kyoto government that I belong to that ken, and will henceforth become a citizen of Kyoto. Then I can make my religious faith known to the Kyoto government; it will be the very first thing ever done in Kyoto. I think the Kyoto government will present the matter to the central government. If case requires, I will present myself to the central government; then, as I said above, in the meantime, I will work privately for religious freedom among the radical statesmen. I think this is the only way to get Kyoto open for our Christian Institution."

Aug. 24th, he writes, " I have already presented the petition for our school, and especially for hiring a missionary, and in order to gain the Governor's favor I made a friendly call on him last night. He strongly advised me to go to Tokyo as soon as possible, or not any later than our petition reaches the central government. I am deliberately following the advice of the Governor who so recently came back from Tokyo and knows exactly the present state of things in the central government."

Mr. Neesima hurried off by jinrikisha overland to Tokyo, and reached there as soon as the petition did. He saw Mr. Tanaka who was at the head of the Department of Education. Mr. Tanaka was Mr. Neesima's special friend, having become such while they were in Europe together. He told him however, at first, that it would be impossible to grant permission for a Christian school to be opened in the city of Kyoto; it was regarded as the sacred city of the empire and he feared great opposition and prejudice on the part of the people. Mr. Neesima saw him again and again, during three days, and Mr. Tanaka finally told him that if he would be very careful not to do anything to arouse the opposition of the people he would grant the permission. Thus the permission was finally granted to open the school in Kyoto. Mr. Neesima also formed a company consisting of himself and Mr. Yamamoto to open the school, hire teachers, etc.; this company of two was the Doshisha for several years.

The present writer having been engaged as the first foreign teacher in the school, Mr. Neesima wrote, Oct. 11th, in regard to a house for my family and one for the school; in this letter he says, "I hope his reply will come within to-day. I think it is pretty early for me to say to-day, it is now 3-30 A.M. I awoke at a quarter before two o'clock, and could not sleep again, so I got up sometime after two o'clock and wrote a pretty long letter to Mr. ——— to get permission to rent his house. Can you do anything for this sleepless old fellow? I am exceedingly tired but can't sleep." Again Oct. 16th, five days later, he writes, "I have been sleepless these past five nights, but I slept first-rate last night. I hope I shall do so again to-night. My hope for Kyoto was quite brightened up." The reason for his brighter hopes was that the permission for my residence in Kyoto, which had been pending so long, and for which he had been writing and telegraphing to Tokyo, had come, and the way was open for him to commence the school. He had had a long anxious summer.

I entered Kyoto with my family Oct. 19th, and settled down in a part of the old Yanagiwara yashiki on the east side of the Imperial palace and Mr. Neesima had a little house on Shin Karasumaru, above Maruta Machi. Mr. Neesima had a small company to whom he preached and taught the Bible in his own house each sabbath all summer; I began a similar service in my house the first sabbath we were in the city, and only six were present, but both audiences increased so that in a few weeks they numbered from thirty to sixty.

We had hardly entered the city, however, before the Buddhist priests held many meetings and finally sent a strong petition to the central government to have us expelled from the city. I find written in my diary of Nov. 19th, "The opposition of the priests is having its effect upon the officials of the city; they are less friendly. The acorn is in the bottle, however, and it will, in time, with God's blessing, split the bottle."

Mr. Neesima made applications about this time for Dr. Taylor and Dr. Learned to teach in the school, and he was very greatly tried for five months before they were granted. I will quote from my diary, of Monday, Nov. 22nd, to show how he was tried. "Mr. Neesima has called several times during the last week or two to see the Governor, but always found him not at home. Friday evening last, he called again, and was told that he was too busy to see him; he went early Saturday morning and was told that it was too early; he went a little later and was told that the Governor was about starting for the office; he inquired through the servant if he could see him in the evening, and was told that he could not promise; he went home, and yesterday he received.

notice to appear at the office this morning and explain what he meant by *Seisho*, Bible, in the list of studies as put forth in the program of the school." The only result of the sending of the strong petition of the priests to Tokyo, so far as we know, was that Mr. Tanaka the head of the Department of Education sent a request to the Governor of Kyoto, asking that, for the present, we would not teach the Bible in the school. Mr. Neesima gave him a written promise to that effect on the 22nd of Nov. The Governor told him that we could teach Christianity in the school under the name of moral science, and teach everything there except Bible exegesis, and that we could teach that and preach in our homes. This request was made by Mr. Tanaka for fear of trouble in the city, as there was great excitement about our coming to open a Christian school. The owner of the building we had rented for the school had given Mr. Neesima notice that he wanted his house for himself, and that we could not have it, but after this Bible teaching was arranged with the Governor, the owner concluded to let us have it.

From my diary, Nov. 29th, 1875. "We began our school this morning in Mr. Neesima's house at eight o'clock, with a prayer meeting, in which all the scholars took part, then going to the schoolhouse, two others were received, making seven boarding scholars and one day scholar." I never shall forget Mr. Neesima's tender, tearful, earnest prayer in his house that morning as we began the school; all prayed from the heart. Dec. 4th, we had twelve scholars. We worked on through the winter, the school growing gradually, until we had about forty scholars; the attendance at the sabbath services increasing, until sixty or seventy were present; the passes for Drs. Taylor and Learned giving Mr. Neesima trouble all winter and finally being sent on to Tokyo and granted in March 1876.

IV.
MARRIAGE, TRIALS, WORK.

"In love of the brethren, be tenderly affected one to another; in honor preferring one another; in diligence not slothful; fervent in spirit; serving the Lord; rejoicing in hope; patient in tribulation; continuing steadfastly in prayer."   Rom. XII. 10-12.

"For marriage is a matter of more worth
"Than to be dealt in by attorneyship;
"For what is wedlock forced but a hell,
"An age of discord and continual strife;
"Whereas the contrary bringeth forth happiness,
"And is a pattern of celestial bliss."   Shakespeare.

"Sorrow and silence are strong,
"And patient endurance is Godlike."   Longfellow.

"Leave God to order all thy ways,
"And hope in him, whate'er betide;
"Thou'lt find him in the evil days
"An all-sufficient strength and guide;
"Who trusts in God's unchanging love,
"Builds on a rock that naught can move."   George Newman.

"Life is real, life is earnest:
"And the grave is not its goal;
"'Dust thou art, to dust returnest,'
"Was not spoken of the soul.
"Let us then be up and doing,
"With a heart for any fate:
"Still achieving, still pursuing,
"Learn to labor and to wait."   Longfellow.

"Blind unbelief is sure to err,
"And scan his work in vain;
"God is his own interpreter
"And he will make it plain."   Cowper.

CHAPTER FOURTH.

Soon after Mr. Neesima came to Kyoto, he met Yamamoto Yaye, a sister of the blind Counselor of the Kyoto Fu; meeting her again and again at her brother's house, he became acquainted with her, and the intimacy rapidly ripened into affection, and in the autumn of that year they were engaged.

On Sabbath. Jan. 2nd, 1876, the Lord's supper and also the ordinance of baptism were celebrated for the first time in the city at the regular service at my house. Yamamoto O Yaye, received baptism at that time, and the next day, Jan. 3rd, in the presence of all the members of our school, of the ex-daimio of Tango and his daughter, of several friends whom we had made in the city, and of Mr. Yamamoto's family, Mr. Neesima and O Yaye were united in marriage. This proved a very happy union, and Mr. Neesima had a faithful, loving wife during all the years until God called him up higher.

In the letters he wrote us from America, while there in 1885, it was very touching to see how much he felt the separation from Mrs. Neesima, and how he also remembered to ask us to help her bear her loneliness.

Mr. Sears, a wealthy Boston gentleman, whose acquaintance Mr. Neesima made while in the United States, sent out a sum of money for Mr. Neesima to use to build him a comfortable home, and also another sum to build a chapel. He secured a large lot on Teramachi above Maruta Machi and there built a home for himself. It was several years before we could secure any places in the city for preaching and a service was held at Mr. Neesima's house and the school met at my house each sabbath afternoon for more than two years. At this latter preaching service more than two hundred people often gathered to hear the Gospel. When the house in which I had lived was torn down, and Mr. Neesima's house was built, the school preaching service and the sabbath school were held at Mr. Neesima's home; this becoming too small, the money given by Mr. Sears was used to build a chapel adjoining Mr. Neesima's house. Mr. Neesima used often to preach in those days, and his

House.

sermons were very impressive; his intense earnestness and feeling impressed all who heard him.

To show the difficulty we met in trying to teach Christianity at this time, one example may be given. A physician in Fushimi, a southern suburb of Kyoto, asked us to come down to his house and teach the gospel; the writer went down one sabbath and gave him and a few of his friends, who had assembled in his house, a talk about the true God; the next sabbath Mr. Neesima went down and talked to the five or six people who assembled; for this, the physician was summoned to appear at the Kyoto-Fu, and told that he must not allow such meetings at his house. All who had listened, or who had received any tracts were also summoned to appear at the office, and very closely questioned and frightened. The physician was summoned for the third time.

The following is a part of the conversation which occurred between the Fu officials and this physician on the last day, when he was discharged. "This Davis came up here to teach an English school, did he not?" "Yes." "Then he is like a man who has a license to sell deer meat, but who sells dog meat." "Well, is it dog meat? I used to think so, but on tasting of it, I find it is a great deal better than deer meat, and I would like to ask you one question ; this way is allowed to be taught publicly in Kobe, in Osaka, and in twenty or thirty places in Tokyo. How is it that here, in the Kyoto Fu, a man is not allowed to hear it in his own house ? Are we not all under the same government ? I do not understand it." " Well," says the official, " I do not say that way is either good or bad, and I do not say that you and your friends cannot hear it in your house, but you let in the common people, the lower classes, who cannot understand it; we cannot allow this. We have good and sufficient religions here in Japan, we do not want any more ; we have Confucianism for the scholars like you, and Buddhism for the masses." The Dr. replied, " I would like to ask you one thing; if Confucianism is an all-sufficient religion, why is it, since its founder lived hundreds of years before Christ, and taught during a long life, that this way has not spread beyond China and Japan ? So if Buddhism is an all-sufficient religion, started by Buddha hundreds of years before Christ, and taught by him through a long life, how is it that it has not spread beyond India, China and Japan ; and if Christianity is a bad way, how is it, since its founder only taught three years, and was put to death when he was thirty-three years old, that it has spread all over Europe and America, and is spreading all over Africa and Asia, and all the islands of the sea?" "Well we do not say that it is either good or bad, but you must not allow people to meet at your house, and you are discharged," replied the official. The 'physician came from the Fu right to my house and told me this at the time and I copied it in my diary. He borrowed a quantity of books and tracts, took them home, and lent them to his neighbors; but his practice gradually fell off, and he came near to starvation, so prejudiced did the people become against him, and he finally lost his interest in Christianity.

This opposition on the part of officials, and the fact that the Bible was not allowed to be taught in the school, caused much dissatisfaction in the Mission, so that after the permission for Drs. Taylor and Learned had been granted, and before they moved into the city, about the middle of March, a special meeting of the mission was called in Osaka, and half a day was spent over the question of abandoning Kyoto, and locating the school where the missionaries could be free to live and to teach the Bible. Although one of the Mission afterwards said it was "the most reluctant vote the Mission ever gave," the vote was given to remain, none dissenting. A few months later, the last of June, a vote was given by the Mission to approve of the erection of two buildings on the ground bought for the school. It was a very reluctant vote; but the fact that most thought it very doubtful if the erection of the buildings would be allowed by the government, helped the doubtful ones, and the vote was given, none dissenting; one brother said, however, "Brethren, you may just as well try to fly to Mars as to try to put up those buildings, it will not be allowed." In just three months and twenty days from that time, this brother sang in the new buildings, "We'll hold the fort," etc., and took part in the exercises of dedication.

As the buildings stood completed, however, and the day appointed to open the school in them drew near, and the temporary restriction in regard to the Bible still held, many of the members of the Mission were greatly exercised about opening the training school of the Mission in the new buildings; some were in favor of demanding the removal of the restriction, and in case it was refused, then of abandoning everything, buildings,

New Chapel. First Dormitories, old Chapel

work and all, and of leaving the city. One brother wrote, "We have no Training school, the school that will begin next week will not be the Training school," etc. Another brothor wrote that he did not believe that we should be allowed to teach the Bible and pray in the school for three or five years, perhaps not for fifteen or twenty years yet.

Within one of a majority of the members of the Mission signed a call for a special meeting to reconsider the whole question of the location of the school in Kyoto, and decide whether we should open the school in the new buildings. Had it not been that one member of the Mission had just started overland to Tokyo and was at this very time weather bound by a three days storm of wind and rain, and wondering why he was permitted to start at all, the meeting would have been called, and no one can predict what would have been the result. But the meeting was not called, and after consultation with Mr. Yamamoto, it was decided, since the excitement in the city had completely subsided, to dedicate the new buildings with religious exercises, to have morning prayers in the chapel, to open all the recitations of the Theological Dep't. with prayer and to teach all the studies and give all the lectures of the Theological

Dep't., except Bible Exegesis, in the new building, and to secure a third building in Mr. Neesima's name, for the Exegesis. The new buildings were dedicated on the morning of Sept. 18th, 1876; they consisted of what are now known as dormitories No. one and No. two. The exercises consisted of a prayer of Invocation, reading the Scriptures, sketch of the founding of the school, prayer of Dedication, addresses in Japanese and English, and the singing of two hymns in Japanese and three in English.

This state of things led to continued criticism of the school, and also to criticism of Mr. Neesima as the virtual Japanese head of the school. He felt these most keenly. He loved the members of the Mission, and he was ever loyal to the Mission, and anything which seemed to imply the contrary pained him beyond measure. So great did the trial become, that in Sept., 1876, the members of the station sent a letter to the Mission to try to remove some of these misunderstandings. I will quote a few words from that letter, as they bring out one of Mr. Neesima's remarkable characteristics. "Still farther, Mr. Neesima and Mr. Yamamoto, as the nominal proprietors of the school, so far from interfering with our management of the school, have from the first left everything in our own

hands; the exercises of the dedication, the manner of conducting morning prayers, what to teach, when to teach, how to teach, the employment of Japanese teachers, the ringing of the bell, the management of the food, all these things, instead of being suggested by them, have been suggested by us, and none of them even referred to Mr. Yamamoto at all, and not half of them to Mr. Neesima, and yet, so far as we know, Mr. Neesima has never hinted or thought a word of complaint, or asked that anything be changed. He even comes to us to consult about all the little details of his own classes. He has not expended a cent of the money which has been sent to him to use as he pleased for the school, without first consulting us, and he has then invariably followed out our suggestions. We have been as free to run the school to suit ourselves, from our first connection with it, as if there had been no Japanese proprietors, or as if it had been located in Chicago". This can almost as truly be said after fourteen years, as after one year.

Mr. Neesima was only anxious that the great purpose of his life should be carried out; in regard to the details, he was willing to yield his way and fall in with the suggestions of others. The first few years of the existence of the school, were years of great trial to him; he stood between the foreigners and the government, and he also stood between the students and the foreign teachers, in some measure. He writes in 1885, referring to these trials, "I often wonder how I came through the deep muds of the past; but I received the sustaining courage and strength of the Unseen Hand.".

We must now notice, at some length, another wonderful work, hardly less wonderful than the calling and preparation of Mr. Neesima. In the month of Feb., 1876, in the darkest days of that first winter, when the opposition was so great that it often seemed as if we must fail of our object of establishing a school in Kyoto, the writer received a large letter by the Japanese post. The handwriting was strange, the name, too, was strange. It was written from the old castle town of Kumamoto, in the middle of the island of Kiushu, by Capt. L. L. Janes. In it he asked if we could receive a number of earnest Christian young men, graduates of his school, into our school, to fit them for work as preachers of the Gospel. We did not know that such a man was in existence; we did not know that such a school was in existence. How did all this happen?

Six months after this, Capt. Janes, while visiting in Kyoto, told the writer of the origin of the school and how he came to Japan.

Early in 1871, the Japanese government wished to secure some one to teach the army the foreign system of drill, and a request went on to Washington for an army officer to come out for that purpose. Capt. Janes was then a Captain in the regular army, stationed in California; he learned that he was to be sent to Alaska, which had recently been purchased from Russia, and he also heard of this request for a man to go to Japan, so he resigned his commission in the regular army and secured the appointment to Japan. Before he reached Tokyo, the government had decided to employ a French teacher of military tactics, and so Capt. Janes was left here, under pay, without any work.

Just before this time, the members of the Jo-i, or foreigners-expelling party, in the old province of Higo in Kiushu, had banded together to start a school to train some men to help oppose all Western ideas and especially Christianity. They had written to Tokyo, asking for a foreign teacher for this school, and the government were glad to send Capt. Janes, and he was willing to go, so in the summer or early fall of 1871, he went with his family alone into this interior city and began this work. He told the writer that so great was the hatred to Christianity, that he did not dare to let it be known that he was a Christian for six months after he began his work there. He made a thorough course of English and Scientific study for the school, covering four years; after six months, he gradually began to bring out the arguments for the existence of a God. One day as he thus made a deduction from science that there is a God, one of his pupils who is now in a responsible position as a Christian worker, said to him, "You lie, sir." After a year or two, Capt. Janes asked the members of the advanced class who could understand some English to come to his house on the sabbath and study the New Testament with him in English; the young men went to their patrons, who were supporting them in the school, and asked them what they should do; the patrons had a long consultation, and finally called the young men and said to them that this school was started to prepare men to oppose Western ideas and especially Christianity, but that in order to most effectually oppose it, they needed to know something about it; hence they might go and learn the Bible with that object. So they went, a few at first, the number gradually increasing until fifteen or twenty went every Saturday evening and Sunday afternoon.

They read through the Gospels in course and the Acts and some of the Epistles, and, as some of those young men have told the writer, Capt. Janes talked to them about the love of God and of Christ, with tears rolling down his cheeks; this went on for more than two years before he saw any signs of yielding on the part of the men before him. Finally the ice began to break up and Capt. Janes sent the letter above referred to. On the 30th of January, 1876, nearly forty of the young men in the school went up on the Hanaoka mountain near the city and signed a solemn pledge, dedicating their lives to Christ for Japan.

No sooner was this fact known, than a great storm broke over the school, the leaders of the Christian band were taken out of the school and imprisoned in their own homes, some of them for one hundred days, and subjected to all kinds of threats and indignities; the mother of one of them appeared before her son with sword in hand and threatened to commit *Harakiri*, if he did not renounce his faith; but they stood firm.

Capt. Janes and his noble wife were the instruments in God's hands to do this wonderful work; and as showing the spirit of the man and also some phases of the work, I will quote from some of Capt. Janes's letters, received during those trying months. In his first letter, dated Feb. 7th, 1876, he says, "My work in the school has been accompanied from the time when it was possible to speak of Christianity, by constant and direct religious instruction of my pupils; in fact, the whole work has been inspired from the first, with the one aim, on my part, of making it, under God, subserve the founding and upbuilding here of the kingdom of Christ, and so the highest welfare of those committed to my instruction, and the large community influenced by them and the school." Again he writes, Mar. 4th, "Meantime, my boys and I have been passing through unusual events to say the least; and the mutterings of a sharp and vindictive and exciting persecution are still in the air around us." "I think the little colony is practically intact; no lives have been taken, tho that was threatened seriously enough; and there are no cases of *Harakiri*, yet to report, tho a mother in one family and a father in another took that method of driving their sons from the faith;

their degradation was declared to be insupportable." "I grieve over my imprisoned Christian boys. The physical strength of one is failing, and the unthinking persecutors may kill him. I understand there was an auto-de fe of his Bibles a few days since."

Again, May 25th, "They blame me here by implication, for educating preachers; I say nothing, but I have come to see that they need preachers and teachers of the 'True Light' more than any other educated workmen. The sham civilisation they would build of a film of Western materialism, dignified by the name of science and civilisation, leaving the soul and all its needs unprovided for, is a hollow bubble that would burst one of these days. It is easy enough to kick a hole through it now; and unless the successive accretions are permitted and made to crystalise around the central principles of truth, justice and liberty,— and a wisdom large enough to satisfy the soul; Christ, the soul's want; God, the soul's author; and immortality, the soul's destiny, why, I don't know but the old nursery style were better than the violent ruptures and fearful reaction that must occur, till the higher plane of progress is reached."

Here are also a few words from a letter Capt.

Janes sent up by the first one of his graduates who started for Kyoto, dated June 25th, 1876, " He was one of the first to see the light, to be convinced of the saving power of Christianity, and to give his heart unalterably to Jesus, 'all to leave and follow him,' and as a consequence, he has been subjected to the most cruel and outrageous treatment at the hands of his weak brother, acting under the influence of the persecuting party here, and an imprisonment of some one hundred and twenty days. He was made the slave of the servants of his family, who were instructed to treat him as a devil possessed, without human rights. He is now, practically, an outcast. He is as a shorn lamb; he is leaving all."

In September, these young men came up, fifteen graduates of Capt. Janes's school, and as many more under graduates, and entered our school; these gradutes were most of them virtually cast off by their friends for their faith in Christ, and they came to us with the clothes they wore and an English Bible, as their sole earthly possessions. They found the school poorly organised and were at first much dissatisfied. Capt. Janes, however, encouraged them to stay, and they remained, and spent three years in Theological study, supporting themselves by teaching the younger classes in the school, and they graduated from the Theological department in June, 1879. Three of them were retained as teachers in the school, and the others went out as teachers and preachers and have been among the best Christian workers in Japan for the last ten years; Mr. Kosaki in Tokyo; Mr. Yebina in Joshu; Mr. Miyagawa in Osaka; Mr. Kanamori in Okayama and Mr. Ise in Shikoku, have done work which has changed the history of Japan already. Five of these men are now connected with the school as teachers. Their coming into the school at that early day with their earnest Christian purpose, gave a tone to the school, and their influence was felt in molding the Doshisha morally and in shaping its course of study from that time. They have helped to make the school what it is, and they came to love Mr. Neesima and be loved by him as brothers.

The school gradually increased in numbers, so that during the third school year, we had over one hundred students; such was the feeling of opposition in Kyoto, however, that we had very few students from the city during the first five years: nearly half of them came from the island of Kiushu, led by the example and influence of the Kumamoto Band.

The opposition on the part of the officials in Kyoto, grew stronger and stronger. Dec. 23rd, 1877, Mr. Neesima wrote, " I wish to inform you of a recent event which happened in Kyoto: my brother-in-law, the blind Yamamoto, lost his connection with the Kyoto Fu yesterday; I believe he lost his connection with the Fu on account of his connection with us." In the winter of 1879, Dr. Learned's permission to reside in Kyoto and teach in the school, had nearly expired; if his permission was not renewed, it would leave only one foreign teacher in the school; the requests made by the Doshisha for others to teach in the school had been refused, and Mr. Neesima was very anxious during those months about the very existence of the school. It was only after repeated solicitation with the Fu authorities here, and a visit to Tokyo and a personal interview with Mr. Mori, then at the head of the Foreign Department, that Dr. Learned's permission was finally renewed.

There were several in the Mission who were opposed during these first years to the plan by which the school was located in Kyoto. It was not strange that this was so; the school was in an interior city where foreigners could only reside on passports which could be withdrawn at any time; the school buildings and homes of the missionaries which were all built with money given by the churches in the United States, could not be owned by the Mission; the government could interfere with the teaching of the Bible and of Christianity in the school; the only wonder, as we now look back, is that any one was found to favour the location of the school in Kyoto under these circumstances. Some opposed the plan of putting the school in the hands of a Japanese company, and some opposed the plan of helping it with foreign money, and it sometimes seemed as if the school would be removed from Kyoto.

The whole situation during these first years was a great strain upon Mr. Neesima. This difference of opinion and agitation in the Mission; the opposition on the part of some of the officials; the refusal again and again of permission for the needed foreign teachers to teach in the school, and the constant fear lest the great purpose of his life should fail, weighed him down. Added to all this was the fact that some of his best Japanese friends told him he was ruining his influence by receiving the money for his support from his benefactor, Mr. Hardy, and advised him to refuse to receive it and try to support himself. He was at one time inclined to yield to the criticisms of his friends and refuse to receive Mr. Hardy's benefaction longer, and it was only by strong urging that he was led to continue to receive it, as needed to help him prolong his life and carry out his great purpose. At one time, when all these trials seemed to be crushing him, he said to the writer with strong crying and tears, "Oh, that I could be crucified once for Christ, and be done with it!" This opposition lasted about six years, and during that time Mr. Neesima was under a strain of great anxiety, most of the time, which seriously affected his general health.

In 1876, a school for girls was opened in the house of one of the missionaries, in which Mrs. Neesima and Miss Starkweather taught, and about two years later, it was removed to its present location in a building erected for that purpose. The care of all this school work, as it grew larger and larger; all the many questions which came up; the requests of students; all difficulties; and the great number of outside calls which came upon Mr. Neesima were a perpetual strain; every difficulty which arose in either school was brought directly to Mr. Neesima, and he must give his time and strength to the settling of it. Then, again, Mr. Neesima's reputation as one of the few men who had been thoroughly educated abroad, and his connection with the Iwakura embassy, brought many callers to his house, and occupied a great deal of his time; he was also consulted in regard to church work and missionary work, and in difficulties which arose in the churches, or between individuals.

His heart was always warmly interested in the rapid spread of the Gospel in Japan, and he made many missionary tours himself, and earnestly proclaimed the Gospel. He wrote from Tokyo, Feb. 13th, 1879, a letter from which the following is a quotation, " I started for Annaka on last Friday morning at three o'clock A.M." This was in the *Basha*, or wagon, which at that time ran between Tokyo and Annaka.—" It was then snowing and I found myself chilled through. I reached Annaka toward evening; although I found myself rather tired, I was obliged to receive quite a number of visitors that evening; then, on Saturday, the visitors poured in from the early morning and there was scarcely a time for me to rest till the evening. We held a prayer meeting on that evening. There were two candidates for baptism;

the meeting lasted more than two hours. Another church meeting was held on Sunday morning. In the afternoon I preached in the usual way and officiated at the Lord's supper. In the evening we held a prayer meeting; it was a very warm and lively meeting and lasted more than two hours. I was so excited by the meeting that I could not sleep at all. At twelve thirty A.M., on Monday morning, I left Annaka on a coach and reached Tokyo at one thirty P.M. I am glad to say that the Annaka church is growing, and before the summer there may be half a dozen candidates for baptism. I have taken cold ever since I went to Annaka." He took this ride of nearly a hundred miles and thus hurried back, because he had had a weighty case of arbitration put into his hands in Tokyo, which he must attend to that Monday afternoon.

Mr. Neesima, during those years, usually attended the business meetings of the Mission, and also the prayer meetings in English of the station, it being held once a week in turn at our houses, his house having its turn with the rest. We shall never forget his simple earnest prayers in English at those meetings. He taught classes in the school in the early years, and he always gained the deep love of his pupils, and of all who came in close contact with him; his silent influence in the school was very strong and pervasive. He also took an active part in the formation of the Japanese Home Missionary Society, connected with the Congregational churches, and had an active part in superintending its work for many years.

V.
BROADENING PLANS; TOUR ABROAD.

" Commit thy way unto the Lord; trust also in him, and he shall bring it to pass." Ps. XXXVII. 5.

" Rest is not quitting this busy career,
" Rest is the fitting of self to one's sphere."

" Build thee more stately mansions, O my soul,
" As the swift seasons roll!
" Leave thy low, vaulted past!
" Let each new temple, nobler than the last,
" Shut thee from heaven with a dome more vast,
" Till thou at length art free,
" Leaving thine outgrown shell by life's unresting sea."
O. W. Holmes.

" In the world's broad field of battle,
" In the bivouac of life,
" Be not like dumb, driven cattle,
" Be a hero in the strife.
" Trust no future, howe'er pleasant!
" Let the dead past bury its dead!
" Act—act in the living present!
" Heart within and God o'er head!"
Longfellow.

CHAPTER FIFTH.

In the year 1883, Mr. Neesima began to think and plan actively to enlist interest among Japanese friends in the establishment of a university, or in the broadening out of the Doshisha into a Christian university. Up to this time the school had only been known in Japan as a Christian school, and the general idea among the leading men in the empire was that it was a school simply for training Christian preachers and evangelists; this was the very natural conclusion from the fact that most of the graduates up to that time had engaged in active Christian work. For this reason it was a very difficult matter to appeal for help for the school; but Mr. Neesima never swerved from his great purpose of a Christian school, nor from stating that publicly in his appeals; it was important to show the public that something besides the Bible and theology were taught in the school, and that its aim was a broader one than simply the training of evangelists, but it was always made very clear that the foundation of the school was a Christian one and that Christianity was the foundation of the morality taught in it.

The writer was present at the first public meeting held for the purpose of awakening an interest in the university among the Japanese; it was held in a large hall in Kyoto in the spring of 1884. About fifty of the officials and leading business men of the city were present and Mr. Neesima, Prof. Ichihara and the writer, each addressed the meeting; those addresses were all strong in their statements that Christianity is and must be the foundation of all moral education. Prof. Ichihara's speech was one of the most ringing appeals for Christianity as the necessary foundation of all education to which I ever listened. The printed appeals which were made later speak for themselves.

The following is a free translation of the first general appeal for the University. It was prepared by Mr. Neesima and Mr. Yamamoto and issued in May, 1884. " The recent political changes in Japan have swept away feudalism which had been the basis of society for many hundred years, and the influence of these changes has grown stronger and stronger until the society of Japan is very greatly changed. It appears like a new Japan. There are many who say that the government, the education, the commerce and the industries which have existed in Japan must be improved. We heartily agree with their purpose as right and important to our civilisation, but at the present time, when we look carefully at the condition of the country, there is one thing which gives us great sorrow. What is that? It is that there does not exist in Japan a university which is founded upon the most pure morality and which teaches the new science. | This is a necessary foundation of our civilisation. In natural beauty and natural advantages Japan is not inferior to Europe and America. Why then is its civilisation so different from theirs? It is also certain that there are in Japan but few noted men of earnest purpose. Hence we need universities in Japan.

"We can learn from the examples which Europe gives us. In the sixteenth century, the great leader, Luther, said, 'If parents or brothers refuse to send children to school, they are enemies of the state and they ought to be punished.' The learned German, Fichte, said, 'The reason that our nation stands first in civilisation among the countries of Europe is in the power which comes from our universities.' The twelfth century was the dawning period of European civilisation. At that time Greek Philosophy was studied in the Paris University. In Italy the ancient Roman laws were studied in the University of Bologna. Between that time and the year 1600, the Universities of Oxford and Cambridge were founded in England, Edinburgh and Glasgow in Scotland, Prague, Heidelberg, Leipsic, Tubingen and Jena in Germany, and Dublin University was founded in Ireland. Besides these, universities have been founded in Holland, Spain, Portugal and Austria.

"Abelard, Roger Bacon, Kepler, Galileo, Lord Bacon, Locke, Newton, Milton, Leibnitz, Kant, Reid and Hamilton were famous in those countries as great scholars. As reformers of politics and religion, Pym, Hampden, Pitt, Fox, Burke, Johnson, Wycliffe, Luther, Calvin, and John Knox were noted. By these universities all science and philosophy have been improved and advanced, by them feudalism and despotism have been destroyed, by them the social ranks and the powers of the nobles and priests have been resisted, by them the desire for liberty and the demand for self-government have been awakend. The English revolution and the religious reformation have occurred, which have completely changed the condition of Europe. In the year 1800 there were over 100 universities in Europe. That the civilisation of Europe has been rapidly advanced by the universities is a most patent fact.

" Now look at the American universities and colleges which number over 300, and of which only eight have been built by the government. Harvard, Yale, Princeton, Amherst, Williams, Dartmouth, and Oberlin are noted, especially the first, which is the most famous one; in it are now 110 professors, and a library containing 134,000 volumes and its endowment amounts to 14,854,372 dollars. In 1872 there were in the United States 298 colleges and universities, but during the seven years to 1879, 66 were added. This great growth of higher education in the United States is a very wonderful thing in the world.

" In the year 1620, the Pilgrim Fathers landed in Plymouth; they came that they might enjoy freedom to worship God. They established a school which was founded upon Christian morality. Since that time, during 260 years, their descendants have inherited the spirit and carried out the purpose of the fathers; they have believed that such schools would diminish the number of evil doers, and increase the number of those who do good; that they would encourage the spirit of liberty and become the foundation of the state ; they have believed that in order to become a nation with the best free government they must have universities which are founded upon Christian morality, where the sciences will be taught. We cannot doubt but that their free institutions have been the result of this spirit.

"As soon as our government saw the importance of the university, it established one in Tokyo, and it has also built several academies. From these we shall see some intellectual development and external advancement, but not moral development and internal improvement.

"Some are trying to improve the morality of the people, but they demand that the old morality of China shall be used with the people, and hence we cannot rejoice at their efforts, for the Chinese morality has not influence upon the mind of men generally. All oriental states are almost destitute of liberty and Christian morality: they cannot therefore rapidly advance in civilisation. The growth of liberty, the development of science, the advancement of politics and the power of morality have brought forth the European civilisation.

These four important effects have come from the study of the advancing sciences upon the foundation of Christian morality.

"We cannot believe, then, that without morality and science, civilisation can come in Japan. To put the foundation of our state upon this foundation is just like putting the foundation of a building upon a rock. No sword can conquer it; no tempest can break it; no waves can overcome it. If it is put upon the old Chinese morality, it will be just like putting it upon a sandy beach of the sea; when the rough waves beat against it, it falls into ruin. We are therefore hoping for a university which is founded upon pure morality and which teaches modern advanced science. We have been very earnest in this matter. In the eighth year of Meiji, we established the Doshisha school in Kyoto, and its purpose was to teach European science and to give also moral education. Its students have increased year by year. But our aim has ever been to build a university.

"In April of the 16th year of Meiji, we publicly expressed our purpose and received much encouragement; at this time we met our friends in Kyoto, and named it the Meiji University. We have determined to raise an endowment first for a department of History, Philosophy, Politics and Economics, and gradually to found one also of Law and of Medicine. But it is not easy to establish this, for we must, as a first step, get a large amount of money with which we can erect some buildings and call some professors. We, being so few in number, cannot furnish this money, but we cannot give up our purpose to establish this university now. We must work for new Japan. All true patriots should do this. Please help us, as far as you are able, to accomplish our purpose and do this work. Unless we receive your help, we cannot succeed in this great purpose."

In the early part of 1884, it became evident that the strain of the last nine years had so exhausted Mr. Neesima, that he must have a complete change. He had tried in vain to rest in Japan; he could not escape from the many calls which pressed upon him everywhere; he could not forget the great work he had undertaken; it was always before his eyes and upon his heart. He at last yielded to the earnest solicitations of his friends, and accepted Mr. Hardy's generous invitation to go to the United States by way of Europe, and on the 6th of April, 1884, he started from Kobe on his long journey. He landed in Italy at Naples.

His daily journals from the time of leaving Japan, until he left Switzerland, are very full; they are little encyclopedias of information on every subject; it is wonderful to see how much information he gathered, and especially, are they very full on the educational side. He visited all the schools and colleges he could, and minutely inspected their whole plan of teaching, studies and buildings, and wrote out all the details. He secured letters of introduction to the men who were at the head of the Catholic Colleges in Italy and inspected them very carefully; also the Waldensian Theological school in Florence. He spent several weeks in the Waldensian valley and carefully studied the history, the persecutions, the school system and the ways of working of that Church. From there he went by the St. Gotthard route into Switzerland; his note books are full of his pencil drawings to illustrate the architecture, and, especially, grape raising, cheese making, etc., etc.

On the 6th of Aug., he started with a German traveller to go up the St. Gotthard pass. It was a gentle climb of about 2000 feet. He says in his note book, "One and a half miles this side of the pass, I began to breathe hard, I could not go; I was left behind; I stopped every ten rods; finally I reached the pass; I ate dinner, but after that I found myself worse and worse; I could not go any farther. I stayed at the hotel Prosa until the next day; that afternoon I found myself very miserable. I thought it might possibly be the end of my life, in this world. While I had a most distressed feeling in my chest, I wrote my will, as follows; First paper; I am a native of Japan, and am a missionary to my native land. On account of my ill health I was obliged to leave my country for health. I came from Milan to Andermatt yesterday, and took a room at the hotel Oberalp. I took a trip to the St. Gotthard pass with a German gentleman this morning; as I found myself too unwell to go on, he left me here and went on to Airolo. I found myself hard of breathing, it must be some trouble in my heart. My goods are left in the hotel Oberalp with some money. If I die here, please send a telegram to Pastor Jurino, 51 Via Torino, Milan, and ask him to take charge of my body. May the kind heavenly Father receive my soul to his bosom. Aug. 6th, 1884. J. H. Neesima. Whoever reads this writing, pray for Japan, my dear native land."

"Second paper; I would ask Pastor Jurino to

bury me in Milan and send this writing to Hon. Alpheus Hardy, 4 Joy St., Boston, Mass., U. S. A., as he and his wife have been my benefactors these twenty years. May the Lord give them ample rewards! Send a telegram to him at once. Please cut a little portion of my hair and send to my dear wife in Kyoto, Japan, as a token of the inseparable bond of union in Christ. My plan for Japan will be defeated; but thanks be to the Lord that he has already done so much for us. I trust he will yet do a wonderful work there. May the Lord raise up many true Christians and noble patriots for my dear fatherland! Amen and amen.

"At this moment all sorts of thoughts came up themselves at once. I reviewed the past as well as the future. My plan for our school; my plan for a medical school; my hope to get something for these plans; my filial feeling toward my aged parents; my tender sympathy with my wife; disappointments of my intimate friends in Japan; my most grateful feeling towards Mr. and Mrs. Hardy; all these feelings and thoughts came up within me and I struggled with them, but I can safely state here that I overcame all these feelings, and prayed to God to let his will be done in me; asked for his forgiving grace through Christ Jesus.

I wrote these above two papers because I was ready to go if it be his will. I had many plans for Japan, but I knew that the Lord cares for Japan more than I. I humbly committed my country's future to his unerring hand. I felt quite submitted myself to his will, but someway tears dropped from my eyes and I could scarcely refrain from it. After I prayed for my soul as well as for the friends who might be left behind, I took a tablespoonful of brandy to prevent my chills, and put a mustard plaster on my chest to prevent my distressed feeling."

He gradually rallied again, so that the next day he was moved in a carriage back to Andermatt; when he was able, he went on to Lucerne, and consulted a physician who told him that his heart was affected and that he must avoid all violent exercise. He travelled leisurely down the Rhine, through Holland and across to England and reached the United States in the early autumn.

Below is a specimen note from his journal, "A short visit to the pastor of Rosa, Italy, Rev. Flugen. I was conducted by a man to his home from the kitchen door. I observed that everything was in an old fashioned style but quite comfortable, neat and snug; I was also led to the dining room which was a large one; a board floor, everything looks simple and unassuming. I saw pictures on the walls; the frames are simple. Some pictures cut out from papers are pinned on the walls. His wife seemed quite intelligent and happy; she dressed simple and neat. His two children looked bright and healthy. Evidently it must be a happy home. He is loved by his people and they are glad to meet and salute him on the street."

Mr. Neesima reached the United States in the early autumn of that year and attended the meeting of the Board at Columbus, Ohio, but he was unable to speak, except a few words. He rested on through that winter, passing some time at the health retreat at Clifton Springs, New York. He wrote from Boston in March, 1885, "Since Feb. 3rd, I have been obliged to lay aside all my reading and writing." This brief letter was written with a trembling hand. He says, "I am still troubled with a burning headache, and have been obliged to keep myself quiet, so far as I can." "I came through this winter without a serious attack of rheumatism, and the only trouble I have now is a burning, heavy headache, with occasional repeats of pain in my forehead. I can't do much yet, but I am not discouraged; I am cheerful and hopeful."

In April and May he made a visit to Washington, stopping in Delaware and other places; but as his health improved a little his soul was wholly absorbed in thoughts and plans for his beloved land. He tried to work for the best interests of the Christian paper in Tokyo; he suggested a revision of the Theological course of study in the Doshisha, to make it more scholarly; he writes from Boston, March 25th, 1885, "The Board are thinking to send a graduate of Ann Arbor University to teach Philosophy, etc., to make the Theological department more attractive to our ambitious students. I hope your mission will heartily respond to this new movement on this side of the Pacific."

His heart was greatly moved also with thoughts and plans for the enlargement of the direct evangelistic work in Japan. He says in the same letter, "I am glad to learn that the work in the Annaka region is so hopeful. They have recently built two more houses of worship." "It may be desirable to occupy a few important centers in Kiushu and in Northern Japan, but the most important work to carry out Christ's kingdom is to raise *men after God's own heart. If you raise up strong and truly pious men to work for Christ, Japan will be ours in his name. Let us unite ourselves* in this case and push it through. I will soon ask a lady in Louisville, Kentucky, to send me sixty dollars to help our needy students."

He was also working to secure a way by which Prof. Shimomura could go to the United States to study, and still further to find some plan by which other men could have the foreign training they needed to fit them to teach in the Doshisha. He says in the same letter, May 26th," With regard to founding special scholarship-chairs in our school, it may be hard to raise fund enough here to secure a few American professorships; so I will work to secure the fund in Japan and raise up the native professorships. In order to do that, a few best students out of our graduates ought to be sent here to pursue the special studies to fit themselves for this new enterprise. I am strongly convinced that we can't keep up our reputation in future, unless we provide a few professional studies besides Theology, so I am hoping to secure a few scholarships to help our students to attain the high education in this country. We may meet many objections here and at home, but I feel we are rather compelled to take this bold step. If we could get a few scholarships here to educate and fit our students to be professors, we could start a few new chairs, on Political Science, Philosophy, History, etc., without a great expense to us. The government is doing this in the Tokyo University, why cannot we do the same in our school? I hope our friends in Japan will raise money enough for us to start this new enterprise.

"To sum up my view, let me briefly state as follows: 1. Give our students a thorough English course. 2. Make the Theological course more attractive to our ambitious students to enter in. Let the foreign professors devote their time and strength for instructing this important class. 3. Provide for other professional studies to keep those boys, who will not become preachers, within the sacred walls of our school. 4. If I secure a few scholarships, I should like to use them exclusively for the best students, intellectually and spiritually, among the Theological graduates. This provision will certainly make the Theological class honorable and attractive in our school. Under this fourth heading, I should say still further; I called on President Porter another day and asked him of his view on my new plan to secure a few scholarships here. He favors this idea very much. I have been working quite hard to secure some favor for our students, very few in number, in the

Johns Hopkins University and also at Yale and Amherst. I hope they will show some special favor to our students if we send them our best specimens.

"Before I close my letter, allow me to state to you that in all these my attempts, I forget myself, I still suffer in my head, I feel that I am moving onward in our battle field just as you do, though I am sent here to rest." At the close of this letter he says, "I cannot write such a letter without shedding many tears. My heart is constantly burning like a volcanic fire for my dearly beloved Japan. Pray for me that I may rest in the Lord. Yours in the Lord, Joseph H. Neesima."

Before he left the United States, Mr. Neesima wrote, "An Appeal for Advanced Christian Education in Japan," which was circulated in the United States, of which extracts are here given.

"Old Japan is defeated. New Japan has won its victory. The old Asiatic system is silently passing away, and the new European ideas so recently transplanted there are growing vigorously and luxuriantly. Within the past twenty years Japan has undergone a vast change, and is now so advanced that it will be impossible for her to fall back to her former position. She has shaken off her old robe. She is ready to adopt something better. The daily press so copiously scattered throughout the Empire is constantly creating among readers some fresh desire and appetite for the new change. Her leading minds will no longer bear with the old form of despotic feudalism, neither be contented with the worn-out doctrines of Asiatic morals and religions. They cried out for a constitution a few years ago, and have already obtained a promise from the Emperor to have it given them in the year 1890. The pagan religions seem to their inquiring mind mere relics of the old superstition.

"The compulsory education lately carried out in the common schools, amounting in number to almost thirty thousand, is proved to be a mighty factor to quicken and elevate the intelligence of the masses. The Imperial University at Tokio is sending out men of high culture by the hundred every year to take some responsible positions either in the governmental service or private capacities. Another university will soon be founded by the government at Osaka, the second important commercial city of the Empire, to accommodate the youths so anxiously craving the higher education. It will be out of the way for me to dwell here upon the material progress Japan has so recently made. But let it suffice to state that the waters of her coasts are busily plowed by her own steamers. Public roads are constantly improved. Tunnels are being cut here and there, and railways are being laid to connect important commercial points. Telegraph wires are stretched throughout the whole length and breadth of the Empire. Surveying what she has accomplished within so short a period, we cannot help thinking that she is bound to adopt the form of European civilisation, and will never cease until she be crowned with success in accomplishing her national aim.

" In order to bring about the recent change and progress she has painfully sacrificed her precious blood as well as her vast treasure. Indeed, her victory has been dearly purchased. It was a quick work, and was well done. It was a sudden movement, but to our great wonder, very few mistakes have been made in her past course. She has tried her best as far as her capacity would allow. The most serious period of our political revolution is nearly passed, and society as well as the government will soon precipitate into some new shape. But what shape? To the writer of this article our immediate future seems a more serious problem than the past. The question is necessarily rising among us, what will be our future? True! She is destined to have a free constitutional government. She is bound to have her people thoroughly educated. It will be a grand achievement if a free constitution and higher education be secured to her people. But these two factors may be proved to be the very elements apt to bring out freedom of opinions, and hence the terrible battles of free opinions. A fearful national chaos might be her fate if nothing intervene to prevent it. If the nation be allowed to take her own course as she does now, hope for her regeneration might forever be gone. But in the time of need, Providence, which rules the nations with infinite wisdom, has stepped in to save us from this national calamity and despair. It was neither too soon nor too late when the missionaries of the cross from America landed on our shore to proclaim the soul-saving gospel to the people. Through their earnest labor and constant prayers the foundation of the Christian church was soon laid.

"We believe Christianity is intended to benefit mankind at large. Why should we not undertake to extend our influence toward the higher sphere, as well as toward the lower, that we might win all men to Christ? Why should we seriously object to raise up Christian statesmen, Christian lawyers, Christian editors, and Christian merchants, as well as Christian preachers and teachers, within the walls of our Christian institutions? It is our humble purpose to save Japan through Christianity. The souls and bodies of our Orientals ought to be thoroughly purged, and consecrated to Christ for establishing his glorious kingdom in the earth as in heaven. If we do not raise up men after God's own heart in the different spheres of our society to leaven the whole lump, we fear the seed of destruction will be soon sown by other agents while we make this delay. Remember what our Saviour said in Luke xvi : 8 : 'For the children of this world are in their generation wiser than the children of light.'

"There might be some undue fear that such a provision of those higher studies would naturally draw away ambitious students from the Theological course. It may be, but we trust we shall receive a larger supply of students in the Academical course, so that some could be spared for other studies without much loss to the Theological department. On the contrary, we may possibly attract some students to it from the other courses.

Some evil may arise in such an undertaking, but it may be overbalanced by the good accomplished by it. Now allow us to state a few reasons for this undertaking:

1. Such a provision will detain the youths for further studies in the school after finishing the Academical course. It will help them to develop and strengthen their Christian character.

2. Such a provision will accommodate some thoughtful parents, who may naturally desire to send their boys to a school where their moral character is carefully fostered and will be likely to be developed so strong as to be a safeguard against youthful vices and corruption.

3. The youths who have thus received a broad culture will certainly have a grand opportunity to influence society for good. Words and deeds of well-educated, earnest Christians in different spheres of society will help the cause very much either directly or indirectly. Sometimes indirect efforts produce more speedy results than direct.

4. This provision will surely benefit and tone up the Theological course, instead of causing any serious harm to it.

5. We desire to lay down a broad basis for Christian education by encouraging post-graduate studies.

"The time is just ripening for us to take this step so as to attract thereto the best and most talented youths in the country and foster and fit them for the highest good and noblest purpose. We are thus compelled to attempt this broad sweep to reach and win thirty-seven million precious souls to Christ. Seeds of truth must be sown now. Undue delay will give a grand chance to unbelieving hands to make thorough mischief and render that beautiful island empire hopelessly barren and fruitless. O Japan, thou the fairest of Asia! 'If I forget thee, let my right hand forget her cunning and let my tongue cleave to the roof of my mouth.'

"As I mentioned above, a movement was started at Kyoto last year to raise some money to found chairs for those special studies. But our friends are very few yet. The people are now pressed hard on account of the business stagnation, and a most destructive flood lately visited the country. So we cannot expect to receive from them any large donation. When we met a number of the eminent citizens of Kyoto last year for this specific purpose, we urged them to give us a fund before the year 1890 so that when the Emperor gives us a constitution in the same year, we might found a

University to commemorate the most extraordinary period of our political history. This appeal created among them a great enthusiasm. Some of them gave us their hearty pledge to do their share. So we may possibly realize some gift just sufficient to support a few native professors. But it is beyond our expectation to receive a fund large enough to sustain even a few American professors. So if a few professorships should be given by some American friends to found chairs of Political Science, History, Literature, Philosophy, etc., it will help the cause grandly. Some people in this country may hardly realize how dangerously our shores are visited and washed by the strong tide of modern European unbelief. But to a native of the country, who has been seriously watching and observing the course recently taken by the people, the present time seems grave. The future battle in Japan may not be with any foreign invaders. But it will certainly be between Christianity and unbelief.

Shall we remain at peace and unequipped because God would fight for us for his kingdom's sake? We fear he will not help us unless we do our part. It is the time for us to make an extraordinary effort to push evangelical work as well as Christian education in Japan in order to save her from corruption and unbelief. The American Board has done for us in the educational line as much as it can wisely do. Yet there remains much to be done in order to carry out our work more efficiently. The Lord's army must not be hampered there while the battle is fairly commencing. Strong means must be provided there in order to furnish to the field strong men from time to time.

"Now who will step forth in this grand republic of America to render us timely help to save us from this impending national calamity? Here may be some friends seriously considering how their property might be best disposed of for benefiting poor humanity. With such we would earnestly plead and loudly cry, 'Remember us.' Would that God might touch the hearts of some individuals to give us a portion of their blessings, and establish chairs for advanced Christian education there as a perpetual monument of peace between the United States of America and Japan, through which the millions of our people and their posterity might be blessed."

In the autumn of 1885, Mr. Neesima returned to Japan, somewhat improved in health, but still suffering from weakness and headache. He at once began to work quietly here for the establishment of the University. He made many earnest friends for the enterprise, and many sums of money were promised toward its endowment. This quiet work and the issue and circulation of small circulars in regard to the University, continued during two or three years, but it was not until 1888 that a public and determined effort was made for the endowment of the University. About six hundred and fifty of the officials, scholars and leading business men of Kyoto, assembled in one of the large temples in Kyoto, and were addressed by Mr. Neesima and others, and much interest was aroused in behalf of the Doshisha University.

In the summer of that year Mr. Neesima went to Tokyo and worked in the interest of the University. So great was his weakness, however, that one evening as he met a few friends to present his plan of the University, he fainted quite away. In July of that year, however, Count Inouye, late Minister of Foreign Affairs, gave a dinner one evening to men of rank and wealth, inviting Mr. Neesima to be present, and after dinner he introduced the subject and asked Mr. Neesima to speak of the University, and the result was, that Count Inouye subscribed one thousand yen, Count O-kuma, one thousand yen, Viscount Aoki, then

Vice-minister of state, five hundred yen, a prominent banker six thousand yen and others enough to bring the amount up to 31,000 yen. This gave great enthusiasm to the movement.

How was this result secured? Mr. Neesima's connection with the Iwakura embassy in 1872, in America and Europe, called the attention of the leading men of the empire to him; then the continued opposition to the school during the first few years of its existence compelled attention; the eyes of the empire were upon the school to see what its aim and outcome were; so, when the school sent out such a class as that which graduated from the Theological department in 1879, the fifteen men who came up from Capt. Janes' school, and the government saw them take such positions and do such work as Mr. Kosaki has done in Tokyo; Mr. Yebina in Joshu; Mr. Miyagawa in Osaka; Mr. Kanamori in Okayama; Mr. Ise in Imabari and as Mr. Ichihara and Mr. Morita did as teachers in the Doshisha, and saw others taking positions as teachers, or as a clerk in a department of state, or as an attaché of a foreign legation: when they saw another class of thirteen go out from the Theological department and take positions as earnest pastors and teachers, when they saw the graduates of the Collegiate course nearly all stable, moral men, taking positions as teachers in schools, or entering their own University in Tokyo, and helping to give moral tone and character to that, they were impressed with the importance of the Doshisha for the Empire of Japan.

When the tenth anniversary of the founding of the school was celebrated in 1885, the Governor of the Kyoto Fu, the Governor of the Shiga Ken and many other officials were present, and were greatly interested. Count Inouye had also visited the school and addressed the teachers and scholars, assembled in the chapel. It was not from any blind impulse that this money was given; the school had proved its right to be, and that it was a needed power in Japan.

In the last English letter which Mr. Neesima wrote, only a few days before his death, from which a long quotation has already been made, he says, "Since 1884, I began to hope for founding a Christian university; the matter seemed to myself and also to my friends here that I am hoping for something altogether beyond hope; however, I had a strong conviction that God will help us to found it in his own name's sake. In order to engage in such an undertaking, one shall need a

Recitation Hall.

strong physique; alas, my health has been poor for some years. When I made a speech before six hundred and fifty select audience at Kyoto, in a large Buddhist temple, in behalf of the new University, I had hardly strength enough to do it; then I came to Tokyo to beg for the fund; I did faint away when I did see a few choice friends at the study of a certain gentleman. The chief trouble was in my heart, a heart disease. I was obliged to confine myself for sometime. As soon as I became comfortable enough, I attempted to move around again. In a single evening thirty one thousand yen were subscribed to us, a most memorable evening to us; it took place in the latter part of July, 1888. Since then subscriptions came from the different parts of the country. At present we have raised over 60,000 yen. We are now attempting to raise it up to 100,000 yen before this coming summer. Since October, I have been away from home, moving round here and there, though I made Tokyo the headquarters of my present movement.

In the latter part of November I became seriously ill; I have not yet fully recovered my strength, and am now obliged to rest at a quiet country town to regain certain strength to attempt beggings further. My humble idea of founding a university is to educate the coming race in higher studies, being influenced by Christian light and Christian conscience. We would put our best strength to Theology, then to Philosophy, Literature, Science, Law, Political Economy, etc. We have had chairs for Theology for some time. Lately, we have secured 100,000 dollars for Science; we are further waiting for funds to come to found some studies, one by one. *It is a faith work.* When you find spare money either in yourself, or in your friends, please remember us. I have a full hope that my vague day-dream for a Christian university will sooner or later be realised, and that in some future, we shall find a grand occasion to give thanks to Him who has led us and blessed us beyond our expectation. Please remember me to your sabbath school friends and ask them to pray for our country."

In this connection, we should speak of an appeal for the University which Mr. Neesima prepared in the autumn of 1888 and which was published simultaneously on the 10th of November of that year in twenty of the leading papers of Japan. This plea for a university is worth reproduction here; being, as it were, his last message to Japan.

Science Hall.

Broadening Plans; Tour Abroad.

"About twenty years ago, at a time when our country was greatly excited over the question of intercourse with foreign nations, having the desire of studying in Western countries, I went to Hakodate, and from thence, in violation of the law which forbade Japanese to leave their country, I succeeded in getting passage on a merchant-ship, and arrived in Boston after a year of hard life as a sailor. In Boston, happily for my purposes, I was welcomed and aided by a well-known American gentleman, by whose kindness I was enabled to study in Amherst College and Andover Seminary. During the more than ten years of my student life in America, observing the conditions of Western civilisation and having opportunity to meet and converse with many leading men, I became gradually convinced that the civilisation of the United States has sprung by gradual and constant development from one great source, namely, education, and also I was led to reflect upon the intimate relation between education and national development. Hence it came to pass that I resolved to take education for my lifework and to devote myself to this undertaking.

"In the fourth year of Meiji (1871), while I was studying at Andover, Mr. Tanaka, minister of education, came with the late Mr. Iwakura, ambassador, to observe the condition of education in Western countries, and I received an official invitation to accompany them for this purpose. After visiting the famous academies and universities of the United States and Canada, we traveled in Germany, France, England, Scotland, Switzerland, Holland, Denmark, and Russia, and I had opportunity to carefully examine the state of education and the condition of the schools in these countries. The result was that I became more and more convinced that education is the foundation of Western civilisation, and that in order to make our Japan a nation worthy to be counted among the enlightened countries of the world we must introduce not only the externals of modern civilisation, but its essential spirit. Accordingly I was the more strengthened in my resolution to establish a university after my return to my home and thus to discharge my duty to my native land.

"In the seventh of Meiji (1874), I was about to return to Japan, and was present at the annual meeting of the American Board and made a short address at the request of many friends: I said that my country was in a disorganized condition, that the people were wandering in search of a light which might guide them into the right way, and that true education was the only means by which the people could make progress both in knowledge and morality. In speaking of this I was so much moved that I could not refrain from shedding tears. Taking one step more in my speech, I said that on returning to my native land I should surely devote my life to educational work, and begged my hearers to help me, if they approved my purpose. No sooner had I thus spoken than a number of ladies and gentlemen in the audience signified their approval of my request by contributing several thousand dollars on the spot.

"Thus the Doshisha was established; and its purpose was, not merely to give instruction in English and other branches of learning, but to impart higher moral and spiritual principles, and to train up not only men of science and learning, but men of conscientiousness and sincerity. This we believe can never be attained by one-sided intellectual education, nor by Confucianism, which has lost its power to control and regulate the mind, but only by a thorough education founded on the Christian principles of faith in God, love of truth, and benevolence to one's fellowmen. That our work is founded upon these principles is the point in which we have differed from the prevailing views on education, and owing to this we failed to gain the sympathy of the public for a number of years. At that time our condition was very weak, with almost no friends in the whole country, with our principles of education not only despised by the ignorant, but treated with contempt even by men of enlightenment. Nevertheless, being convinced of the ultimate victory of truth, helping and strengthening each other, we proceeded on our way with a single eye to the end and with strong determination amid the greatest difficulties.

"Fortunately general opinion has now changed respecting religion, so that even those who do not themselves believe in Christianity are ready to acknowledge that it contains a living power for the regeneration of men. Thus society has been prepared to welcome us. At the same time our Doshisha has come to be appreciated and respected, and people have begun to recognize that we are giving our students a sound and well-balanced education both intellectually and morally, so that our school is one to which parents may send their children without hesitation. Meeting with such favorable reception, our school has steadily advanced both in number of students and in grade of its curriculum, and ever our friends have urged us to furnish higher and higher courses of study.

"Especially in the fourteenth and fifteenth years of Meiji (1881 and 1882) such requests began to come in upon us, and we felt that we must proceed to lay the foundations of the future University. Yet the establishment of a university is one of the greatest works that can be undertaken in this country, one in which we need many helpers and much money; and what was our condition at that time? Having a few friends and helpers, we were not so entirely neglected as at first, but still we were in an isolated condition. What then could we do? Yet never for a moment did we falter in working for our purpose. We sought those who might favor our plans and help us, and, finding several who gave us assurances of aid, we held several meetings, to which we invited the members of the Kyoto Fu Assembly and asked their coöperation. Receiving the approval of the leading members of the Assembly, we published a tract, "On the Establishment of a Private University," and set forth in it the purposes of the proposed institution. This may be called the first step in the undertaking of the work. Nevertheless, although many gentlemen gave assurances of help, as it was a time of business depression, nothing was accomplished towards raising money, and our plans seemed to come to a stop for a while. Also I was obliged to go to America for a time and to leave the work in the hands of friends during my absence, so that the whole amount raised until April of the present year (1888) was only about 10,000 yen.

"During the present year we have especially devoted ourselves to this work, and good results have been accomplished. In April we called together over six hundred of the prominent people of Kyoto and explained our plans to them, at which time Mr. Kitagaki, the governor of the Kyoto prefecture, not only approved our purpose, but himself made an address urging the people to help in the work. Since then several meetings have been held and a committee is collecting money, and we have reason to hope that our confidence in the generosity and public spirit of the people of Kyoto will not be disappointed.

"And I have worked in Tokyo as well as in Kyoto. Counts Okuma and Inouye and Viscount Aoki and others, to whom I have explained my plans, have expressed their approval of them, and especially Counts Okuma and Inouye, after visiting the school and personally inspecting its working, have given it their warm recommendation and encouraged us in our purpose of establishing higher courses of study. Besides these, other gentlemen and business men of Tokyo and Yokohama, after hearing my plans, have given the following sums since April of the present year:—

    Count Okuma . . . . yen 1,000
    Count Inouye . . . . ,, 1,000
    Viscount Aoki . . . . ,, 500
    Mr. R. Hara . . . . . ,, 6,000
    Mr. K. Iwasaki . . . . ,, 3,000
    Mr. K. Okura . . . . ,, 2,000
    Mr. H. Tanaka , . . . ,, 2,000
    Mr. Y. Shibusawa . . . ,, 6,000
    Mr. Y. Iwasaki . . . . ,, 5,000
    Mr. H. Hiranuma . . . ,, 2,500
    Mr. K. Masuda . . . . ,, 2,000

"Counts Ito and Katsu and Viscount Enomoto have also signified their approval of our work and have promised to aid us. In addition, some friends of mine in America have promised $50,000 towards the endowment of the present school, and another friend has recently promised $15,000 for a Science Hall.

"In view of this, since our work has now progressed for twenty years or more, and has gained so much approval in many quarters, and since we are now beginning to meet with so much success, I think we must now be diligent to seek out many helpers; for the institution of a university is a great undertaking, and needs much money and help of all kinds. Such an opportunity as we now have, if once lost, may never be found again, and therefore we must not waste a moment. Also when we consider the present state of the Doshisha we feel sure that our purpose is not in vain. We have increased the number of trustees of the Doshisha Company, perfected its constitution, and thus established the government of this educational work upon a firm basis. At present we have a Preparatory course, an English Collegiate course, a Theological course, a Girls' School, and a Hospital and Nurses' School. The following table gives a few statistics in regard to each :—

	Regular teachers.	Assistant teachers.	Pupils at present.	Graduates.
Preparatory department,	1	13	203	108
Collegiate department,	17	6	426	80
Theological department,			81	57
Girls' school,	13	2	176	21
Nurses' school,	3	2	13	4
	34	23	899	

Library Hall.

"The school has thus attained so advanced a position that we expect to make the course of study in the collegiate department equal to that of the government's *Koto Chiu Gakko* (colleges) within the present year. We feel, therefore, that it is necessary to add the university course to the present school; that the time has come for the establishment of the university. Since the university is the place for thorough training in special studies, those who graduate from our Collegiate department should have university courses open to them to carry on their studies in such special departments as they wish. To leave the Collegiate department without the higher courses of the university is like building an arch and leaving out the keystone. Thus we are sure that the establishment of the University cannot be postponed. . . . .

" What is the true end of education? We understand it to be the full and symmetrical development of all our faculties, not a one-sided culture. However much students may advance in the arts and sciences, if they are not stable and persevering in character, can we trust them with the future of our country? If, in consequence of principles of education which shoot wide of the mark, our young men are molded and trained in a one-sided and distorted manner, no one can deny that such principles are extremely injurious to the country. Such students, in their search for Western civilisation, choose only the external and material elements of civilisation—literature, law, political institutions, food, and clothing, etc.—and seem not to comprehend the source of civilisation. Consequently, blindly groping for light and wandering in darkness, they are misled by selfish and erroneous principles in the use of their acquired knowledge. And though there come some who wish to reform these evil tendencies in education, they only make the evil worse by resorting to measures of oppression and restriction instead of training up noble and high-principled students whose minds are free and broad as well as disciplined, and who govern th.mselves and follow the right way with self-determining conviction. We would hold our peace were it not that these thoughts make us anxious for our country and people.

"We think that Western civilisation, though many and various in its phenomena, is in general Christian civilisation. The spirit of Christianity penetrates all things even to the bottom, so that, if we adopt only the material elements of civilisation and leave out religion, it is like building up a human body of flesh only without blood. Our young men who are studying the literature and science of the West are not becoming fitted to be the men of New Japan, but are, we regret to say, wandering out of the true way in consequence of their mistaken principles of education. Alas! what a sad prospect this offers for the future of our country! We sincerely confess that we are of ourselves unworthy to undertake so great a work, but, with God's blessing and the help of our patriotic fellow-citizens, we will forget our own weakness and even venture upon this great task.

" To express our hopes in brief, we seek to send out into the world not only men versed in literature and science, but young men of strong and noble character, by which they can use their learning for the good of their fellowmen. This, we are convinced, can never be accomplished by abstract, speculative teaching, nor by strict and complicated rules, but only by Christian principles,—the living and powerful principles of Christianity,—and therefore we adopt these principles as the unchangeable foundation of our educational work, and devote our energies to their realization . . . .

"This being my purpose, when I consider my own strength I find it far short of accomplishing so great a work, but I cannot be silent; the needs of our country and the urgency of my friends forbid me to decline this task. Thus being stimulated and urged on by the condition of the times, forgetting myself, I devote myself to this work, and I pray that with God's grace and the help of my fellow-citizens this University may be successfully established."

Early in August, 1888, after the money mentioned above had been secured for the University, Mr. Neesima became so weak that some physicians in Tokyo told him he had only a short time to live; one other physician told him that if he took complete rest for two years, he might possibly live on several years. He went to Ikao, a health resort in Joshu, on a mountain side, rented a small cottage and spent nearly two months there. He was so weak when he went up there that he was unable to ride in a jinrikisha and was carried up in a kago or bamboo chair. When the writer visited him in that place in September, he had just become able to walk out a few rods. His stay there helped him to a little strength, and in October he returned home, but soon went to Kobe, where he could have more complete rest; he spent most of the winter in Kobe, in great weakness.

Early in the year 1887, a plan of union between the Congregational and the Presbyterian churches in Japan was proposed. Mr. Neesima was consulted but very little in regard to this plan beforehand, probably on account of his ill health, but when a copy of the proposed basis of union came into his hands, he was greatly troubled. When he came to talk with me about it, he was more excited than I had ever seen him before, and more troubled than I had seen him for many years.

Mr. Neesima had become greatly impressed during his residence in America with the value of freedom; he felt that Japan needed freedom, and that it could come most safely only gradually and among those institutions which, like the Christian churches, were under the influence of men of strong moral convictions. He wanted to retain the leavening influence of the Congregational system. Differing with the experienced pastors, his former pupils, who had assisted in preparing the basis of union, he felt that the plan proposed by the committee sacrificed that principle of freedom too much, and hence he said that he must oppose it; he feared the effect of his opposition upon the Doshisha, but he said he could not yield this principle, even at the risk of severing his connection with the Doshisha and with the Kumi-ai churches. He even suggested that if the union was perfected on the basis first proposed, that he might leave this part of the country and go to the Hokkaido and work alone. I encouraged him to patiently wait and see if the proposed basis could not be modified.

In the following months, although some of his best friends told him he would ruin his hopes for a university by his course, and caused him great anguish of heart, he maintained his position, that unless the proposed basis was materially modified, he could not favor it. This was a very great strain upon him during many months, and a strain which he could ill afford to bear, in his weakness.

With the spring of 1889, Mr. Neesima seemed to regain his strength in some measure; he spent sometime during the summer at a seaside resort, quietly resting, and he was there when the news came to him that his Alma Mater, Amherst College, had conferred upon him the degree of L. L. D. He wrote at this time a very characteristic letter to a member of our Mission. He said that he was greatly troubled because they had conferred upon

him this degree. He had always refused any position which had been offered him in his own country, and he felt he was not worthy of this title, and he ends by asking, " What shall I do with it?" He was the first one among his people to receive such a title, and he was worthy to receive it.

The Doshisha had been growing all these years; the Girls' School had increased its buildings and more than doubled its numbers; the Training School for Nurses had been established; a Preparatory department had been added to the school for young men; the first two dormitories had increased to thirteen; a large recitation hall, a chapel to seat six hundred, and a large library building had been erected, the three latter all of brick. A gentleman in New England, Mr. Harris, had gradually become interested in the work which the Doshisha is doing, and had written that he was glad to take into consideration a plan to do something for the school, and this resulted, first in his giving fifteen thousand dollars for a Science hall, and during 1889 his interest developed into his making his gift 100,000 dollars to endow the Science department of the Doshisha. Mr. Neesima saw the foundations of this new hall laid before he went to Tokyo, in October, 1889. The students had also increased so that during the school year of 1888-9 there were in all departments of the Doshisha, over nine hundred young men and women.

VI.
LAST DAYS OF WORK, SICKNESS, DEATH AND BURIAL.

"*For I am already being offered, and the time of my departure is come. I have fought the good fight, I have finished the course, I have kept the faith: henceforth there is laid up for me the crown of righteousness, which the Lord, the righteous Judge, shall give me at that day: and not only to me but also to all them that have loved his appearing.*" 2-Tim. IV. 4-6.

"*So live that when thy summons comes to join*
"*The innumerable caravan that moves*
"*To that mysterious realm, where each shall take*
"*His chamber in the silent halls of death,*
"*Thou go, not like the quarry slave at night,*
"*Scourged to his dungeon; but sustained and soothed*
"*By an unfaltering trust, approach thy grave*
"*Like one who wraps the drapery of his couch*
"*About him, and lies down to pleasant dreams.*"   Bryant.

"*Having won by toil and pain,*
"*Who shalt regret the pangs of life?*
"*Who would regret the past's long night.*
"*With all its fear and chill and blight,*
"*If now the East, through twilight gray,*
"*Were streaked with everlasting day?*"

"*The things o'er which we grieved, with lashes wet,*
"*Will flash before us out of life's dark night,*
"*As stars shine most in deeper tints of blue.*"

"*So let the eyes that fail on earth*
"*On thy eternal hills look forth;*
"*And in thy beckoning angels know*
"*The dear ones whom we loved below.*"   Whittier.

"*He does well who does his best;*
"*Is he weary?   Let him rest!*
"*Brothers!   I have done my best,*
"*I am weary—let me rest.*"

"*Say not good night,*
"*But in some brighter clime,*
"*Bid me good morning.*"

CHAPTER SIXTH.

The autumn of 1889 found Dr. Neesima far from well, but yet able to be doing some work. He expressed a great desire to go to Tokyo and work for the University. His physician told him that he felt it would be better for his health not to go at all, but if he was not absent more than three weeks, it might not do him any harm. He went to Tokyo in October, and saw a great many friends in that vicinity, talking of the University endowment, and receiving many promises of aid. He also visited Joshu, and while there, he caught a severe cold which confined him to his bed for a week, and left him so weak that he finally determined to go to Oiso, a quiet place on the sea shore near Yokohama, and rest. He went there in December, and took a room in a common Japanese hotel. He was accompanied only by his clerk. Mrs. Neesima had intended to go and spend sometime with him there, but his mother was taken sick in Kyoto, and as she was eighty four years old, it seemed unwise to leave her.

The new year came, and Dr. Neesima sent out many New Year's letters to his friends, and especially to the leading pastors and workers; in one of these he said that the greastest need of the church in Japan for the new year, was a *new baptism*, so that we might be prepared to take Japan for Christ. He sent an acting pastor in Niigata a letter nearly three yards long, urging upon him the importance of planting workers in the important centers of that province; he sent another similar long letter to a man in the extreme west end of the empire urging the planting of the Gospel in that region.

Professors Kanamori and Shimomura spent the night of Jan. 10th with him, and they talked over various plans for the University, the School of Science, etc., and Mr. Neesima seemed as well as usual.

In his last English letter, written Jan. 5th, 1890, he says, " In the latter part of October, I became seriously ill; I have not yet fully recovered my strength, and am now obliged to rest at a quiet country town to regain certain strength to attempt beggings further."

Jan. 11th, he began to feel poorly, and he grew

Death and Burial. 133

worse from day to day, so that on the 17th, one of the best Japanese physicians in Tokyo was summoned to see him; he pronounced his disease peritonitis, and said that he was a very sick man; his clerk, who was with him, wanted to telegraph immediately for Mrs. Neesima, but Dr. Neesima said, "No, wait a little." On the morning of the 19th, Mrs. Neesima was sent for by telegraph, and she arrived the 20th, in the evening. Mr. Kosaki, Mr. Tokudomi and other friends had already reached his side from Tokyo.

The first word which came to Doshisha was given to the school on Tuesday morning, January 20th, and Mr. Kanamori, the Acting Principal of the School, started that day for Oiso. The word given to the school was "Kitoku," "very dangerously sick." Little circles of men were praying for the life of him they loved all that day in the school, and in the evening a general prayer meeting was held in the chapel to pray for him; the telegrams came, in the same words, "Kitoku." That prayer meeting was the most touching meeting I ever attended. Such tearful pleading with God I never heard before; some of the prayers were almost demands, but most of them contained the, "If it be thy will."

The next day no better news came, and the praying went on and others of the teachers and students started for Oiso; Thursday morning came the telegram, " No hope," then a little later, " A little hope now," and at a quarter to five P. M. just as the teachers were assembling for their Faculty meeting, the word was passed around of his death. No business was done but to appoint a committee to arrange in regard to the funeral, and recitations were suspended until after the funeral.

Dr. Berry reached his side three hours before the end came. He was conscious to the last and was able to talk some, up to within a few hours of his death. While he was yet able to converse pretty freely, he had dictated his last words to his friends, in regard to the school and to the Missionary Society. As he came to the last words about Mission work, he had maps of five provinces spread out before him, maps which he had been studying before. He called for colors with which to mark, and they brought a saucer with three colors on it to his bedside. With these colors, he marked out the strategic points on the maps, one color for those which should be soonest occupied, another for those of next importance in the campaign, and the third for the next. As he did this he became so excited and animated over it that his friends had to check him. Early Thursday morning, he asked his wife and all the friends who were with him to come in and he bade each one an affectionate farewell; from that time on he spoke very few words; everything was done and said that he wished to say; his soul was at rest, and he was simply waiting to go; he gradually sank and at about twenty minutes past two o'clock, Thursday afternoon, Jan. 23, he breathed his last.

A mattress and bedding had been secured for him a day or two before he died, but he said that he came into the world in confusion, and he was not worthy to die so comfortably. The last passage of scripture which he asked to have read to him, a few hours before he died, was Ephesians, third chapter. This was read, friends prayed with and for him, and he was at rest.

The following is a free translation of a poem Dr. Neesima wrote as he entered upon the new year. "As the old year goes out, I leave its sorrows behind. In bodily weakness I hear the early cockcrowing, ushering in the new year; although I am of little worth, and my plans for the salvation of the people have been deficient, yet now with a greater aim, will I enter upon the new year."

Among the farewell words, penned at his side just before he died, are the following. To Mrs. Hardy; "I am going away; a thousand thanks for your love and kindness to me during the many years of the past, and also for the fine presents you sent me lately. I cannot write myself; I leave this world with a heart full of gratitude for all you have done for my happiness." To Dr. Clark; "I want to thank you most sincerely for ,your confidence in me, and in all I have undertaken. I have been able to do so little, owing to the delicate condition of my health."

The following are free translations of others of his farewell words. In regard to the Doshisha; 'The future object of the Doshisha is for the advancement of Christianity, Literature and Political Science, and for the furtherance of all education. These are all to be pursued together as helping each other. The object of the education of the Doshisha is not Theology, Literature or Political Science in themselves alone, but that through this education, men of great and living power who love true freedom, may be trained up, men who shall live for their country." "The

Trustees should deal wisely and kindly with the students. Strong minded and bold students should not be hardly dealt with, but dealt with according to their nature, so as to develop them into strong, useful men. There is danger that as 'the school grows larger, it will become more and more mechanical, hence this should be carefully guarded against." " The utmost care should be taken, that the foreign and Japanese teachers may be united together in love, and work together without friction. I have many times stood between the two, and have had trouble. In future, I ask the Trustees to do the same as I have done." " I have not desired to make a single enemy, but if there are any who feel inimical toward me, I ask such to forgive me, for I have not the least ill feeling in my heart toward anyone." " The work which has been accomplished is not mine but yours, for I have been enabled to do it only through your earnest coöperation; so that I do not regard it as my work at all, and I can only most sincerely thank all those who have so zealously worked with me."
" Do not find fault with heaven, nor blame men."
" My feelings in regard to the Doshisha are ever like this poem; " In time of cherry blossoms in Mt. Yoshino, morning by morning, my great

anxiety is lest a cloud come and destroy the view."

By a curious coincidence, Dr. Neesima was born on the 14th day of the 14th year of Tempo, and he died on the 23rd day of the 23rd year of Meiji. The body reached the Kyoto station by rail from Oiso, at half past eleven o'clock, Saturday evening, and the whole school were at the station to meet it. The school was formed in line of march, the Preparatory students in front, and the classes in order, ending with the Theological classes in the rear. The Preparatory students began carrying the bier, as many as could take hold of it, and they changed at each corner, so that when we had reached the house, all had had a part in bearing the loved body. It was a scene never to be forgotten; a light snow was falling; snow covered the ground, melting into slush, but there were very few of the nearly seven hundred students who were not in line that night, and when we reached the gate of Dr. Neesima's house, two and a half miles distant from the station, before we entered, one of the teachers made a very touching prayer, one of the petitions of which was, that in all the funeral exercises we might do as our departed brother would desire.

On the Sabbath, the casket was open in the house,

and all the students and teachers of the Doshisha schools, and hundreds of others viewed the face they loved. A memorial service in Japanese, three hours long, was held in the chapel in the forenoon, and one two hours long in English, in the afternoon. The funeral was on Monday, the 27th. A large tent was extemporised by covering poles with tent-flies, in front of the College chapel, and all the seats from the chapels and recitation rooms of the school were placed in it so that three thousand people crowded into the tent, and about one thousand more stood outside. About fifty huge bouquets of flowers, arranged with branches of evergreen, nearly five feet high, stood in line from the gate to the entrance of the chapel. The casket was covered with flowers in beautiful designs, and a large table in front was also covered with wreaths, anchors, etc., etc. The service was simple; hymns; reading the third of Ephesians, the last passage Dr. Neesima had read to him; two tender prayers; reading a brief history of his life; and Mr. Kosaki preached a short and very appropriate sermon from John XII, 24.

The funeral was attended by all the members of the schools; by the Mercantile school which marched up in a body; by about seventy graduates of the Doshisha, who had come from all parts of the empire; by hundreds of Christians from the city and hundreds from outside the city, as well as by many hundreds of others, including the Governor and many officials of the Kyoto Fu, the Governor of the Shiga Ken, a delegation of Buddhist priests from Osaka, and by many members of his own and of other missions.

At half past two o'clock, in a pouring rain, the procession formed; the students again acting as bearers; they had insisted from the first that no one outside of the school should touch anything; they assisted in digging the grave; they now bore the loved remains to their last resting place, and carried all the fifty or more large bouquets, the banners, etc. The procession reached nearly from Imadegawa to San Jo Dori— a mile and a half—, it went down Teramachi to San Jo, east on San Jo to the side of the mountain, and through the beautiful Buddhist temple grove where the body of Dr. Neesima's father rests, and where burial was refused for Dr. Neesima's body, because he was the "very head-centre of Christianity in Japan," as they said, and then wound up the mountain to a most beautiful spot, overlooking the city and the mountains and valleys beyond. Many banners were borne in the procession, including one from Osaka, inscribed, "From the Buddhists of Osaka;" one also from Tokyo on which was inscribed one of the last utterances of Dr. Neesima, "Free education, Self-governing Churches; these keeping equal step; will bring this nation to honor." Many from the school also; among the inscriptions in English were, "Remember me," "There is a happy land," "Yet I live," "The Truth shall make you free," etc. At the grave, two hymns were sung, a prayer was offered, and the benediction closed the exercises.

The earnest, tried soul is at rest; he has heard the welcome, "Well done thou good and faithful servant, enter thou into the joy of thy Lord." He is in the midst of that joy, while we strive to finish the work which our loved brother began to do, the foundations of which he so well laid.

The great company of mourning friends who assembled from all parts of the empire at his funeral, and the hundreds of sympathetic telegrams which came from leading men, show how wide was the influence of this great commoner. Viscount Aoki, Minister of Foreign Affairs, sent a letter saying, "I have lost a great and good friend." Count Inouye telegraphed to those at his sick bed, "You must keep him alive." He still lives. Tho dead, he still speaks to this whole nation.

VII.
MEDITATIONS, CHARACTER, LESSONS.

"*Blessed are the dead which die in the Lord from henceforth yea, saith the Spirit, that they may rest from their labors; for their works follow with them.*" Rev. XIV. 13. "*Except a grain of wheat fall into the earth and die, it abideth by itself alone; but if it die, it beareth much fruit.*" John XII. 24.

"*Humility is the base of every virtue.*"
"*God keeps all his pity for the proud.*"   Bailey.

"*Hath any wronged thee? be bravely revenged:*
"*Slight it, and the work is begun; forgive it, and ' tis finished.*"

"*Good must ever live, and walk up and down the earth, like a living spirit, guided by the living God, to convey blessings to the children of men. It lives in humanity, in some form or other, like the subtle substance of material things, which tho ever changing never perishes, but adds to the stability, the beauty, and the grandeur of the universe. The influence of the holy character also passes beyond the stars, giving joy to our angel brothers; and to our elder Brother, Jesus Christ, who in seeing his own love to his, and our God, to his neighbor and ours, reflected in his people, beholds the grand result of the travail of his soul, and is satisfied.*"   Macleod.

"*Some soul shall reap what we have sown in tears.*"
                                            Laura B. Boyce.

"*They never quite leave us—the friends who have passed*
"*Through the shadows of death to the sunlight above;*
"*A thousand sweet memories are holding them fast*
"*To the places they blessed with their presence and love.*"
                                            M. E. Sangster.

"*Lives of great men all remind us*
"*We can make our lives sublime,*
"*And, departing, leave behind us*
"*Footprints on the sands of time—*

"*Footprints that perhaps another,*
"*Sailing o'er life's solemn main,*
"*A forlorn and shipwrecked brother,*
"*Seeing shall take heart again.*"   Longfellow.

CHAPTER SEVENTH.

The most difficult part of the writing of this sketch of our brother, is the right estimate of his character; we are asked in what his greatness consisted? Although he had mental power above the average, that was not the secret of his power; although he had fair executive ability, this, also, was not the secret of his great success. He went to the United States and had extra advantages given him, so that he came back to Japan when there were very few among his countrymen who had similar advantages, but neither was this the great secret of his power. There was a deeper, a more subtle, and more important secret of his power and success than all these.

Before attempting to analyze his character, I want to give a few meditations found in his notebooks written in Europe and America in 1884-5, and a few extracts from letters which he has written during the last fifteen years; these extracts could be multiplied almost indefinitely. The following were written in his journal, July 24th, 1884, while in the Waldensian Valley, Italy.

"There is great danger of our forming an opinion of others by looking at them in one case. We should be careful, because some are quite deficient in one thing, tho they may be quite efficient in other things. There must be some defect found in a so-called perfect man. In the first place, Find his temper; 2, His education; 3, His surroundings; 4, His circumstances or situation in life; 5, See him, how he behaves in some unusual case.

Never criticise too soon; surely we shall misjudge him. Judge him with a Christian grace. Never be too harsh or too minute; love him as our heavenly Father loves us. If we have love on our side then we may lose all our petty, criticising spirit. Oh! it is a most unhappy and unhealthy thing to have too critical eyes for others. The best way will be not to judge others, as our Lord has taught. When we discover some defect in others, take it as if it were upon us, and try never to repeat it again. When we see great success among our brethren wish more success for him. Never look upon our dear brethren with envious eye. If he is good, praise him, pray for him and follow his example. I often observed that when some one heard good news of his friend, some one would say, 'But he is so and so,' instead of rejoicing over his success. There is a weak human nature prevailing everywhere. There is a great deal of competition among educated people. Note; Be specially patient when we are sick or are feeling unhappy."

It is wonderful to see this man, who had himself come out of darkness only a few years before, while travelling in dark Italy alone, write down such meditations as fill his journals during those months. Here are others of the same date, July 24th. "Silence." "Silence is one of the virtues. There is much safety in silence. Wise men never talk much; as our mouth and tongue were given to use for good purposes, use them for good purposes. Vain and senseless talking often injure our reputation and cause us to lose our manhood. I often noticed uneasiness and chaff-like element in some vain, talkative men. There is something noble and secure in silence. Silence is a manly forbearance. A man of silence is a blessing to a family or to a society. Silence ought by no means to be combined with a bitter countenance but with a cheerful countenance. Vain talking often disturbs affairs in a family or in society, but silence heals it. We can easily weigh a man of vain talk, but we could not easily measure the depth of the mind of a wisely silent man. But do not keep silence, if we can by talking do much good to others, or for the truth. Oh, how large a portion of our talk we spend for vain things of the world, and how little for the truth! When a word goes out of our mouth it is like spilled water on the parched soil, there is no possibility of taking it back again; what is said is said; it becomes a fact of our lives for which we must give account in the future. But above all, let us not harbour evil thoughts, for evil thoughts are the main spring of evil and vain talking."

Same date, "Poor creatures: we plan much and do very little. Our plans are often defeated by something." Same date, "Receive others patiently. If any one imitates a hero, let him be so, receive him well. If any brother do not behave as he ought, let us wait for some occasion to drop a kind word, so as not to offend him. Never send away a brother in Christ when he comes and seeks our friendship. Bear the evils of others for God's sake, for he bears our evils patiently. He does not correct us furiously, at once, but uses many occasions to heal us and takes many years to sanctify us. But let us by no means neglect our duty toward others. Look at the ocean, how beautifully it looks! Yet it must receive many filthy matters from the shores; it receives and purifies them. We shall be happy men if we can be like it. Be minute for ourselves in everything, but when we come to deal with others, let us be careful not to offend them with a close calculation."

Same date, "Don't be Jack-at-all-trades. In passing through some country towns, I notice that there are ever so many things spread and shown in shops, but when I closely examined each article, I found that each kind is rather scanty. It is well for us to be widely informed on many subjects, but do not imitate these country shops; many articles with a scanty supply of each. We ought to be well posted at least in one subject of the professional studies. It will be a rich treat to us. Success in our life will chiefly hang upon it. Let this be our offensive or defensive weapon on the battle field of truth. Tho our talent may be small, yet it is solid and weighty. *Be single minded for a single purpose.* We shall sooner or later reach our mark. Never shoot our arrows into the air, aim at an object surely, and then let it go. If we miss, then repeat the process again and again until we can satisfy ourselves. I never knew a single case of a talented, puffed up, yet unsettled minded man having accomplished anything noteworthy."

Same date, "Never miss a rare occasion to do good. Let our guns be always loaded. When we meet our game, aim at it and shoot it instantly, for our game will never wait for us. When we meet any occasion to do good to others, then don't let it go. Don't wait for tomorrow, do it at once, for we may never have the occasion again. To shoot wild game is a mere pleasure, but to shoot men for our Master is a grave business. Let our guns be first loaded with living powder and bullets from on high and be always ready. Many hunters of men carry their guns unloaded; this explains the reason why Christ's kingdom among men does not spread faster." Same date, July 24th. "At my sick bed."

"The Divine Fire." "Many Christian ministers may have highest culture, and may write their sermons with much skill and thought; beautifully executed work, like a Grecian marble statue. Alas! there is no heat in it. Heat must be caused by fire; if there is no fire in the sermon to heat the hearers' hearts, it is a serious affair; Divine fire is needed for heating man's heart. This fire can only be got by daily seeking. Those who depend very much upon their talent and knowledge, are very apt to forget to seek this much needed Divine fire for themselves, as well as for their hearers. How cold such a heart must be to a congregation: it is fireless and lifeless. If each professing Christian has this Divine fire, what will be the aspect of the Christian world? If each has this fire, Christ's kingdom will come much faster. Oh! heavenly Father, give us this fire! However small we may be, if we have genuine fire, we shall consume even the whole world. How small a spark of fire burned up a vast forest in Canada! How small a lamp light consumed two-thirds of the great city of Chicago! Sometimes one may make an artificial fire in imitation of the Divine fire, but his hearers will sooner or later detect it; it is a mock fire. God will not bless such. Oh, let the Divine fire be burning within us always.

Same date, "Man's Greatness." "Man's greatness is not simply in his learning but in his disinterestedness in self. Those with much learning are apt to be more selfish than the unlearned. Let us look at Christ on the cross. He is our example. Oh, how noble, how grand, how gracious he seems to us! Let us forget self, and offer ourselves freely for the cause of truth and good. Let us also be truly penitent and humble. I call this man's greatness."

The above meditations were written in one day, when, after going up on a mountain excursion from Rosa in the Waldensian valley, he says, "We passed one night in the mountain house. I sent my thick coat and shawl with a donkey, and the donkey did not come that evening. I had to go without my shawl; I slept under the hay; uncomfortable." The result was that the next day, July 22nd, he had a fever and it took him two days to get back to Rosa again. His entry for the next day after his return, July 24th, is, "I was quite unwell; called Dr. Vala; he gave me quinine once in two hours." Yet on this day, "At my sick bed," he wrote the meditations, above given.

Here follow other meditations from his journal. "A thought for preaching." "Suppose the future Judge of the moral world comes down now and summons each of us to appear before him, and uncovers all our past deeds before the congregation, how many of you will dare to step forward and get all your deeds eternally penned upon the walls of the sacred edifice to be read by each of you?"

"Human Happiness." "God gave us a sense of happiness so that we might be truly happy. It is right for us to feel happy when anything is given us from Him. Let us be happy for the daily bread we receive, happy for pleasant circumstances, good home, good friends, pleasant situation, etc. But all the earthly happiness will become as nothing at all when we are permitted to step though the gate of Paradise and catch the glory of the Lamb of God, who caused the gate of Heaven to be opened to us; let us aim at this happiness; this, only, is abiding."

"Promises." "Fulfill your promises promptly; never postpone it till tomorrow, for we may not see it, or may be fully occupied with something else; then we shall have no occasion for excusing ourselves for the delay. It is a sort of weakness and sham for a man to make all sorts of apologies to another; let yea be yea and nay be nay. Do, or not do. Never be sluggish, and never leave business half done."

"Business Character." "The Italians appear to be polite, but they lack business character. They are easy and like to be easy. They would rather postpone their business if they can. . They will not move unless they are pushed by some one. Do your business promptly when it is required to be done. Do not waste your time by talking; do it at once and it is done." "Try to talk what we mean, but never talk anything which we do not really mean in our heart. It is a moral weakness to say what we do not really mean. Straightforwardness can be found mostly among the Anglo-Saxon races, English and Americans."

"Roughness and Politeness." "A rough manner with a kind heart is far more preferable than a petty politeness with no least meaning. Japan is one of the politest nations in the world, but, alas! their heart is far from it. Artificial politeness became the national habit. This is not the result of true sincerity. Politeness ought to be a necessary exponent of true love and kindness, but politeness without a least meaning is a sort of deception." "Remember that we are always naked before Him who does never slumber nor sleep."

"Watchfulness." "Watch, pray, and be prepared for the Master's call. We know not when he will come, whether in the first watch, the second watch, the third watch, or the fourth."

"A policy for our Training School." "Let us be like an unpolished diamond, never mind the outward, rough appearance, if we can have a shining part within. Let these three factors be our perpetual mottoes: 1. Christ as our foundation stone. 2. Well qualified instructors. 3. Well selected library and thoroughly equipped apparatus. Those three factors will be true and shining parts of our Training School. Too much of brick and mortar does not suit my humble taste. I am terribly craving for the inner polish that will be a glory of our school; that will certainly command the respect to the thoughtful Japanese more than brick, stone and mortar."

"The True Hero Worshipper." "Most of the Japanese will be hero worshippers; they are a hard set of people to be managed, except by a hero to whom they can look up. Yet they are very easy to be led away by a hero. They are moved with the sensational currents of the hero's opinions. There is a lack of individuality in them. Most of the hero worshippers will be always colored by the same tint as the hero himself. The weak point is that they do not rise above their hero. If the hero makes a mistake, or failure in his career, they will do the same. If the hero falls, they will fall, likewise. The matter has been so with us when we examine our history closely. You will also find that there has been no hero in Japan who has done all for unselfish ends. He is apt to be more selfish than the common mass of the people. If their mind be directed toward the Hero of heroes, the greatest the world has ever produced, I am sure it would revolutionise the future of Japan. He is far above Socrates and Confucius, yet he is a friend of the poor. He is far above Alexander and Napoleon, yet he shed his own blood for the people, instead of shedding the blood of hundreds of thousands of innocents for his own gratification. He had no selfish aim in his life ; he was perfectly holy and yet perfectly simple ; he had no place to rest his head, yet he sat from eternity on the throne of the universe. If the Japanese are bound to worship heroes, let them worship this Hero, the Hero of heroes. His worshippers will also be tinted with the one best color, that is, the color of godliness. Within this bound, there is an ample scope for freedom ; man can choose any professions except bad and harmful ones. In following and worshipping him, we shall obtain the true human liberty, we shall certainly have our individuality. Oh, how I long that our people should turn their attention on this Hero who is far above weak humanity ! ".

"Questions." "Is there any one in the world who is perfectly above selfish ambition? How can he know himself that he is perfectly free from that? How can we know that such an one is free from it? Is there also any one who is perfectly free from the slightest deception? Could ever deception be eradicated from civilised society? How many of us could say to God that I have lived my life without the slightest ambition or deception? Has any one ever seen, or could we ever expect to see such a perfect type of humanity among the race of Adam, except the Son of God? It is too foolish to entertain such a question. But I would like to meet a person of the above description."

"A Best Method of Teaching." "If I teach again I will pay a special attention to the poorest scholar in the class, then I should succeed."

In a letter from Tokyo, March 24th, 1878, he closes the letter with, "Pray for me so that I may be directed entirely by His hand." After an absence in Tokyo, on his return, he writes, "Kyoto, Monday morning, July 21st, 1879. I arrived in Kobe yesterday at five P.M., and passed the last night in Nishinomiya. I might have returned home last night, but lest I should break the sabbath, I stayed at the above mentioned place. I came home this morning a little after nine o'clock. I have not seen Mr. Yamamoto yet, but I don't believe the present difficulty is very serious. We have the strong God to depend upon. I trust He will make the matter all right."

During the revival at the time of the Dai Shimbokukwai or General Conference, in Tokyo, he writes, "Tokyo, May 11th, 1883. Dear Brethren in Kyoto; I am anxious to write a few lines to inform you how the Lord blessed us in our Dai Shimbokukwai. We commenced it on Tuesday, with a one hour prayer meeting. It was the most impressive meeting I ever attended in my life. A spirit of union was greatly manifested in that meeting; then followed the business meeting; Mr. Miyagawa was elected chairman. In the afternoon we had reports of the delegates; it was a most enjoyable part of the conference. I can assure you that the Lord blessed us far more than we asked for."

While in America the last time, he wrote, dated Boston, March 9th, 1885, closing the letter, thus, "The only trouble I have now is a burning, heavy headache with occasional repeats of the pain in my forehead. I can't do much yet, but I am not discouraged. I am cheerful and hopeful.

I trust you are praying for me. Pray for me, so that I may no longer live for myself but only for my Master."

Again, when he had heard news affecting the Doshisha which greatly troubled him, he writes from Dorchester, Mass. March 22nd, 1885. "We shall be in a hard fix then. I know not what to say, but I can only state to you that *I am on my knees.* I hope I shall get a further light upon this serious subject." In the same letter, he speaks of the great trials and difficulties of the past, and says, "I often wonder how I ever came through those deep muds of the past," but he adds, "I received the sustaining courage and strength from the unseen Hand," and again, at the close of the same letter, "Recently I learned something from experience, when I meet any serious or alarming case, I keep myself *stand still*—, not to be frightened by them; afterward they pass off all right." Again, when serious misunderstanding had arisen in regard to Mr. Neesima's action, and a letter had been sent to him which he calls, " The most insulting letter I ever received in my life," he writes from Milford, Delaware, in regard to it, April 20th, 1885, "I am sorry to say that his letter is thrown into the waste basket. When I read it, I said within myself,

'What! have I lost a sense of honor?' but I knelt right down for God's grace to preserve me, in his hand. I am all right now, please don't mention it to any one." "I thank God for his ever sustaining grace to me. Each trial and each difficulty draws me nearer to his hand; he sustains me and helps me far beyond what I can ever know or discover. Pray for me that I may be ever nearer to him." May 26th, 1885, he closes a long letter of ten pages written from Boston, which is full of plans for the school, and for the spreading of the work in Japan, with, "Pray for me that I may rest in the Lord." When starting for Tokyo in August 1875 to try and get permission to start the Doshisha, he closes his letter with the words, "Pray for my success."

Dr. Neesima had a deep vein of humor in his nature. I remember that the first time we came to Kyoto, in June 1875, to look at the land for the Doshisha, we visited the San Jiu San Gen Do, a Buddhist temple where are a thousand life-size wooden images. As we walked among them, Dr. Neesima said with a laugh, "These images are just fit to keep poor students warm in the winter." A missionary once sent a very *cheap* kakemono, or wall-picture, to a friend in America. When

Dr. Neesima was in the United States the last time, he visited this friend, and was shown this article over which a great deal more ado was made than the article warranted; he was asked to explain it, and he told the missionary who sent it, after he returned to Japan, "I read all the characters except the price mark; I thought," said he, with a twinkle of the eye, "you would be willing I should omit that." Only a day or two before he died, when his wife and one or two other friends were changing his clothes, and causing him to groan with the severe pain, "Oh how you hurt," he said with a groan, and then added, "This is the first time I've ever been stripped by *good* people."

Dr. Neesima told one of our number the following incident of his early boyhood. His father was rather strict with him and one day whipped him severely on his hand; this made him very angry, so that he sulked and would not speak to his father, so after a day or two his father called him to the little garden, pointed to a delicate bamboo, called the sasa and recited this poem, "Nikunde wa utanu mono nari; sasa no yuki." "I do not strike in anger; snow on the sasa." As snow bends and almost breaks the delicate sasa, we must tap it gently so that it will rise erect again. By this Dr. Neesima felt touched, knowing his father's love for him, and he ceased his sulks. When Dr. Neesima began the study of the Dutch language in Tokyo, he needed a dictionary, but he had no money, so he opened his father's money drawer, took out eight yen and put in its place a paper saying he had taken it and would replace it sometime; when the money was missed and the paper found, Dr. Neesima said that he had borrowed it, and that he had to run in debt two yen more to get the dictionary, whereupon his father gave him the balance of two yen.

Miss. Isabella Bird describes her visit at Dr. Neesima's home in her " Unbeaten Tracks in Japan," Vol. II, page 232-235. She says, "Mr. Neesima is a gentleman to begin with, and has quiet, easy, courteous manners. He is a genial, enlightened Christian and an intensely patriotic Japanese. He gives a sad account of the lack of truth and the general corruption of morals among his countrymen. I asked him what, in his opinion, are the leading faults of his countrymen, and he replied without a moment's hesitation, 'Lying and licentiousness.'"

Dr. Neesima was present at the opening of the

branch sabbath school, in a large pottery in the southern part of the city of Okayama in the fall of 1880, and was invited to preach the first sermon. In it he emphasised the need of being pure in heart, and told of seeing in America a beautiful and and costly Japanese vase which the gentleman had recently purchased. He admired and praised the workmanship to the gentleman's satisfaction, but when asked to explain the designs, he hung his head. " There " said he, " were the signs of our country's shame, the designs were too vile to be told."

Dr. Neesima's character contained the principle of love to a marked degree. He had strong love for his friends and it was a love which was broad as well as deep. He deeply loved the students of his school, and this love was universally reciprocated by the students. He loved them so much that it almost broke his heart to have any of them leave the school on account of dissatisfaction, or to have to send any one out of the school as a punishment. He could hardly bear to exercise discipline in the school. On one occasion during the earlier history of the school, some grave offences had been committed, and yet Dr. Neesima felt that the school was partly to blame, or such things would not happen, and instead of punishing the offending students, he said the Doshisha must be punished; so, one morning at prayers in the chapel, he stated those convictions to the school, and said that he was going to punish the Doshisha, and he could do it in no other way than by punishing the head of the school, and so, taking a stout withe in his right hand, he struck his left hand a succession of blows which brought the tears to every eye in the house before one of the older students could interfere to stop him. In all his connection with the school, I never heard a student say anything against him, and I never knew that one did so.

Dr. Neesima's love for the members of his own Mission and for all the foreign workers in Japan, was very strong, and they loved him in return. His earnest yet simple and unassuming ways won all hearts and begat a love which no discussions or difference of opinion interrupted. He had the love and respect of all the foreign workers in Japan who knew him, and he had no more sincere mourners at his death than the large company of foreign friends of different Missions who gathered at the memorial services in Kyoto and in other places.

Another trait was peace. He tried as much in him lay to live in peace with all men. He was ready to yield his own view; this was almost a fault with him. He was sometimes too ready to yield to the opinions of others. During all the years of his connection with the school as its President and head, he never once, so far as I know, set up his opinion against that of the teachers; he always yielded and worked in harmony with them. He was always ready to yield any point which he felt was not contrary to the great aim of his life; when that was at stake, the whole world could not move him. He was generally a joyful, cheerful man. His strong faith and hope kept him in an atmosphere of joy. So, too, we might speak of his long-suffering, gentleness and goodness, also of his faith; in the darkest hours, his faith in God and in ultimate success only seemed to grow stronger.

His meekness was remarkable. He was from the first the head of the school, and yet, during all those years, he kept himself in the background and never insisted on his rights as President. It was hard work to get him to take the President's seat on the platform in the chapel.

When, however, we go deeper and seek the main-spring of these graces, we find as the Apostle tells us in Gal. V. 22, 23, that they were all the

"Fruit of the Spirit." The main-spring of Dr. Neesima's character and the secret of his great success was in his union to God in Christ through the Spirit. He felt with Paul, "I can do all things through Christ who strengtheneth me."

It is difficult to analyse the great secret of his power and success, but we may mention a few points.

1. Loyalty to duty. From the day he read of the Creator in the little Chinese Geography, to the day of his death, his loyalty to duty shines out. As soon as he gained an idea of God, he felt his obligation to him and he began to discharge it, and as the months and years went on and his vision of duty broadened, his sense of obligation broadened with it, and efforts to discharge that obligation kept pace with his enlarging vision. No matter what were the circumstances, and no matter how great the loss, he was always loyal to the higher duty. Take the example of his travels in Europe with the Embassy; he would stop off and spend the sabbath alone.

2. He took a great aim and one which was in harmony with God's great aim. He did not take a low aim, he did not take a selfish one; he took for his aim the establishment of a great Christian

University, for the sake of lifting up so far as he could through that, his whole nation toward God and a Christian civilisation. His great aim was not education for its own sake, but for Christ's sake and as a help to lead the millions of Japan to Christ and eternal life. The results of that school are already changing the history of the empire.

3. He had a holy, absorbing ambition to realise his great aim. This ambition led him to forget himself, and devote his whole being, and all his powers to secure the great aim of his life. He counted not his life dear to him if he could accomplish his great object. When, a few years before he died, the question was raised of his going to the United States a third time to try and secure money for the endowment of the University, and his physicians told him it would be almost certain death for him to go, he replied that that would make no difference with him, if he felt that by going he could secure the money. His going to Tokyo and working during the last months of his life were done in a similar spirit. He wanted to die in the harness, and he did.

4. He committed himself and his great plan and all its details to God, with a firm faith that God would give him success. He never seemed to

waver even in the darkest days. In the last English letter which he wrote, this faith shines out. After speaking of the gift of 100,000 dollars for the Scientific School, just as Prof. Shimomura was ready to return to his work in the school, he says, "Is it not wonderful that when he was about ready to come home, the way to make himself useful was opened before him. Oh dear friend, I am a strong believer in the most wonderful dealings of Providence with those whoever believe in God. As for me, I am a man of delicate health and am not permitted to do much now. However, he has employed this poor and helpless instrumentality to bless others in his behalf." And then in that letter he tells of his "Day-dream to found a Christian College," and how he received no human encouragement, but he says, "However, I was not discouraged at all, I kept it within myself and prayed over it." Then the night before he made his appeal for money at Rutland, he could not sleep, and says, "I was then like that poor Jacob, wrestling with God in my prayers." Then, later, when he took up the larger work of founding a University, he says, in the same letter, "The matter seemed to myself and also to my friends that I am hoping for something altogether beyond a hope, however, I had a strong conviction that God will help us to found it in his Name's sake," and again, "I have a full hope that my vague daydream for a Christian University will sooner or later be realised, and in some future we shall find occasion to give thanks to him who has led us and blessed us beyond our expectation."

5. His heart was greatly interested in direct mission work. Deeper than all other thoughts, more important than all other plans, was the thought and the planning to bring the millions of Japan to Christ. This was fundamental to his whole plan for a Christian College and University. When compelled to rest in the United States, or in Ikao, or in Oiso during the last weeks of his life, he never could rest from thinking, planning, writing and praying over the great problem of the speedy evangelisation of Japan.

When the writer visited him for an hour in Ikao, where he rested in great weakness during the summer of 1888, he was no sooner seated than Dr. Neesima said, "I have someting I want to show you," and he went to the adjoining room and brought out a map, of the province of Joshu, and on it he had marked every place where there was a church, every place where the gospel was regularly preached, and other places for which he was praying and planning to secure evangelists. He had no greater sorrow during the closing years of his life than that which came from the fewness of those from among the graduates of the Collegiate department of the Doshisha who prepared themselves to preach the gospel directly. He was often ready to weep over it as he spoke of it, and he wept as he prayed over it.

He begins his round-the-world diary in 1885 in the following words, "April 6th; Went on board the Khiva at Kobe, accompanied by my wife and other friends. I separated from my wife with prayer, committing her to the care of my Father in heaven, upon whom she can rely far better than upon myself." "April 7th, Monday, Prayer for Theological Students." "April 8th, Came to Nagasaki, 6-30, A. M.; Pray for fifth year;" and so on, day after day, we read, "Pray for vernacular class," "Pray for theological class." He carried this intense desire for workers to be raised up to reap the waiting fields of Japan around the world with him, and presented this object in earnest prayer to God every day.

He always let his Christianity be known; as has been mentioned on previous pages, his first

work when he reached his native land was to preach the gospel to the people in his old province of Joshu; he did it so earnestly that the Governor of the province was alarmed and made a journey to Tokyo to inquire about it; so earnestly, that it has brought forth an abundant harvest. His first work when he came to Kyoto, in 1875, was to start a religious service in his house on the sabbath where he preached Christ to a little company of men and women. The facts of the organisation of one of the first churches in Kyoto in Dr. Neesima's house and that its services continued to be held in his house, have already been mentioned. Dr. Neesima was always and everywhere known as an earnest christian; the impression of him among his countrymen was well voiced by the Buddhist priest of a temple in the eastern part of the city where the body of Dr. Neesima's father was buried, who, when asked for permission to bury Dr. Neesima's body there, objected, saying that Dr. Neesima was the head of Christianity in Japan, and it would not do for his body to be buried there; or by the words of a high official who remarked, when Dr. Neesima had persisted in holding firmly to his Christian principles, "well, you are a *slave* of Jesus Christ, are you not?"

What then, are the lessons of this life to us who remain?

1. Let us realise that God still moves in a mysterious way his wonders to perform in the world. The age of miracles of physical healing may be past, but we have before us the fulfilment at the present day in the world of the Savior's promise, "Greater works than these shall he do, because I go to my Father." The wonderful calling of Dr. Neesima twenty six years ago; his preparation; the bringing of Capt. Janes to Japan and the training of the band of men who should be associated with Dr. Neesima to make his school and his work a success; the bringing to this land of the missionaries who should be associated with him in that work; the planting of the school in Kyoto, in the midst of the great prejudice and opposition, and its success as it stands before the world to-day, is as great a miracle as is recorded in the Old Testament or the New, if we except the miracle of our Savior's incarnation and atoning work. It is simply inconceivable that all these improbable things should happen, and that they should come together at just the right time, simply by chance.

2. Let us all grasp the fact of the greatness of the work which God used our brother to begin. When God called Abraham out of his father's land and home to go into a strange land, he had a great purpose and work to accomplish through him. God does not work such wonderful deeds as this sketch contains without having a great plan and purpose to accomplish through them. We can see already that the Doshisha is changing the history of Japan, and if the plan of our brother can be carried out, this school will be one of the greatest factors in the civilisation and Christianisation of Japan. But if this is to be the result, then all the friends of the school, foreign and Japanese, must realise the greatness of the sacred trust which they have inherited from its beloved President, and with a similar love and faith and hope and patience they must hold the school true to the great purpose of its founder, not education for its own sake, but education for the sake of God's glory and the salvation of men.

3. We may learn that self-denial for Christ is the greatest gain for self; that he "who would be great must be a servant, and that he who would be first, must be servant of all." God takes care of the man who is loyal to him, loyal to his own

conscience, loyal to duty, loyal to right. The happiness and final success and glory of that man follows of necessity, because it is a part of the eternal nature of things, and because God will sooner or later put his approving smile upon that man and upon his work. Dr. Neesima's name will be remembered on earth long after the names of many so-called heroes are forgotten, and his place in heaven will be above that of every man who has sought his own glory.

4. Let us remember that just as Dr. Neesima's life was a plan of God, so every man's life may be a plan of God. If we will but put ourselves in God's hands to be led and used by him and work with God and let God work with us, we shall work in harmony with God, we shall work with God, and our power and ability will be multiplied by an infinite Factor, so that God only can measure, and eternity alone can reveal, the results of our life-work. "The good man does better than he knows!"

"Blessed are the dead who die in the Lord." Dr. Neesima rests from his labors, and his works follow him.

明治廿三年十一月一日印刷
明治廿三年十一月十日出版
（正價金壹圓）

著作者 米國人 ゼー、デー、デビス
京都市上京區烏丸通今出川下ル西側

發行人 上田周太郎
京都市上京區相國寺門前町壹番戸

印刷人 廣瀬安七
東京市日本橋區兜町壹番地 製紙分社

賣捌所 丸善商社書店
東京市日本橋區通三丁目十四番地

www.ingramcontent.com/pod-product-compliance
Lightning Source LLC
Chambersburg PA
CBHW020902230426
43666CB00008B/1275